PRAISE FOR *THE L...*

'Nidhi has touched a fascinating as ... ...
the living patterns of society change, the culture also changes. And
the culture left behind is like leaving behind your reflection on the
mirror when you move away. These stories are like those pieces of
mirrors. They remind me of my own face in the past. *Rudaalis*, dai
maa, *chaarpai-banaane* wallah, *ganderi* sellers, barbers, who also used
to carry matrimonial proposals before they appeared on the Internet.
And many more. This absolutely beautiful piece of writing by Nidhi
Dugar Kundalia is an ode to my past and to many others like mine.'

GULZAR, lyricist and poet, Padma Bhushan awardee

'Nidhi Dugar Kundalia's *The Lost Generation* is an enticing
collection of first-person narratives woven around her unique
encounters with practitioners of rare professions that conjure up a
world on the verge of disappearance. These are nuanced stories of
living people told with delicacy and panache, whose charm comes as
much from the beauty of the minute details as from the power of the
macro narrative. An inviting read.'

K. SATCHIDANANDAN, pioneer of Malayalam modern poetry,
bilingual critic, playwright and editor

'A fascinating collection of essays on India's rare and vanishing
professions—from *ittar* wallahs overtaken by the parfumerie industry
to letter writers outflanked by the mobile phone revolution—
rendered with genuine feeling, an eye for the telling details coupled
with vivid writing, Nidhi Dugar Kundalia's *The Lost Generation* is
an unforgettable portrait of a disappearing India.'

DR SHASHI THAROOR, member of Parliament for
Thiruvananthapuram and Lok Sabha chairman of the Parliamentary
Standing Committee on External Affairs

'This wonderful book is not just a chronicle of India's dying
professions, it is also a powerful portrait of our past. After you finish
reading these compelling narratives, you are certain to look around
for those letter writers and professional mourners with a sense of
longing. *The Lost Generation* is a brilliant ode to ancient India.'

ANEES SALIM, author, winner of the Hindu Literary Prize, 2014

'This book could not be more timely. As India is swept up by the winds of change, we often forget those home-grown traditional family professions, both cruel and kind, which continue to impact the lives of millions. Written in a light, conversational style, Nidhi Dugar Kundalia unfolds those forgotten worlds before us, taking us through cities and villages where technology and modernity are still foreign words, and there is all abiding faith in the power of human relationships.'

KISHWAR DESAI, columnist and author, Winner of the Costa Book Award for First Novel, 2010

'Wistful, well-researched, well-written chronicles of professions and professionals we've left behind on our unrelenting march towards modernization.'

BARADWAJ RANGAN, film critic, deputy editor of *The Hindu*, winner of the National Film Award for Best Critic

'*The Lost Generation* offers a fascinating glimpse into a world that is either wholly disappearing into glorified anachronisms or is being pushed further into the ignored margins of a city. Going beyond the odd magazine feature or the photo essay that hurries to romanticize these professions, Nidhi's accounts dig deeper to place their stories within various social and political contexts. The book is a crucial, much-needed documentation of the times and the ways of life [that are] very different from what a lot of us in India experience in our daily lives.'

DEEPA BHASTHI, columnist

THE LOST GENERATION

CHRONICLING INDIA'S DYING PROFESSIONS

Published by Random House India in 2015
1

Two stories, 'The Boat Makers of Balagarh' and 'The Bhisti
Wallahs of Calcutta', first published in their earlier forms in
Kindle Magazine in 2012, have been reproduced here.

Random House Publishers India Pvt. Ltd
7th Floor, Infinity Tower C, DLF Cyber City
Gurgaon – 122002
Haryana

Random House Group Limited
20 Vauxhall Bridge Road
London SW1V 2SA
United Kingdom

978 81 8400 737 4

Typeset in Adobe Garamond by Manipal Digital Systems, Manipal
Printed and bound in India by
Thomson Press India Ltd, New Delhi

A PENGUIN RANDOM HOUSE COMPANY

THE LOST GENERATION

CHRONICLING INDIA'S DYING PROFESSIONS

NIDHI DUGAR KUNDALIA

RANDOM HOUSE INDIA

*To my grandparents, who coloured my childhood
with their stories*

CONTENTS

INTRODUCTION

I first saw him in Tiretti Bazaar in the early hours of the morning, when it is still possible to walk and observe the activities before crowds throng Calcutta's old quarters. Tea-stall owners juggling streams of tea between glasses; a street barber sharpening his razors against a stone; a beedi maker drying his *tendu* leaves on the cobbled sidewalks. He sat between them, our *bhisti* wallah—the water carrier—before the corporation taps, suspended between old and modern, waiting to fill his animal-skin bags with water. His ancestors, though, would fill their water from the banks of the Ganga and freshwater springs, serving Mughal troops in war fields, the Nawabs of Bengal and then the British. The bhisti wallahs were crucial machinery in ordinary people's everyday lives too—watering the gardens of zamindars, filling pots of water for the nautch girls, offering cool water to worshippers at mosques on the days of Jum'ah (the Friday prayer) and filling cups for weary travellers and thirsty lepers. As the century turned, however, they quickly devolved into mere spare parts, only delivering *mashq*s to those whom the government pipelines had failed to reach. Like the old, abandoned palatial homes of the noblemen dotting this congested market, this solitary bhisti wallah is a testament to significant events and feats of importance from decades ago, but like their deepening cracks and crumbling walls, he is also a stark reminder that, one day, dust only goes to dust.

The streets in the ancient cities of India are suspended in a time warp—not the lofty, shiny lanes of the city, but the old, faded, deceived to-be-pulled-down-any-time-now streets. A perpetual sense of nostalgia lingers in these old neighbourhoods, a sense of belonging to a time you were not born in. Buildings, lives and occupations that were integral to existence in the past still exist here, although you only catch glimpses of these in the cities' decaying old streets, below disintegrating edifices and, often, in the villages on the fringes of the vast metropolises. Bhisti wallahs, beedi makers, wigmakers, postmen, wooden-boat makers, entertainers, storytellers, letter writers, *ittar* wallahs—the professionals who were such an integral part of everyday life centuries ago are fading into oblivion, fast giving up their ancestral professions.

Scribes who manually copied books were replaced by printing presses followed by the computer. Radios and televisions cut into the livelihoods of nomadic storytellers. SMS technology caused the death of letter writers. Much has been said and written about this Disneyfication of the subcontinent, but little has been said about the debris left behind by the globalization that is rapidly transforming the originally diverse and syncretic Indian society. Resultantly, the hapless last generation of these ancient professions have been left wondering about the bleakness of their futures. The scribe who teaches calligraphy at an academy in Delhi told me while we chatted in his class, 'We struggle to make Urdu survive, let alone Urdu calligraphy, in this digitalized world. It is like being on a small raft in the middle of the ocean, drifting on it for days and nights, with the only incentive being more of the same—blue against blue.'

On my travels around India, I found the new and old worlds intersecting in unpredictable ways even as modernization spreads through the country. Outside Vikarabad, in Telangana, I met in a church compound a lady gravedigger who had taken up her father's job—a lower-caste job originally reserved for men—despite protests from her community. On the one hand, her Christian community objects to this feminist stance and, on the other, they lobby and protest outside government offices against caste discrimination, asking to be granted scheduled caste status. The members of the community were originally Hindu Dalits who had converted to Christianity over the years, but the retrogressive practices and prejudices against them haven't changed much. Indian law, unfortunately, does not say anything about 'Untouchable Christians'.

In Jaisalmer, Rajasthan, a midwife, or dai, provides training to other women in midwifery practices because of her distrust in modern birthing practices at today's hospitals. She limits her teachings to traditional midwife castes, which were essentially a lower caste. 'It is to preserve our ancestral professions,' she told me defiantly. In villages, it is not uncommon for affluent families to bestow land grants to a dai's family and give her the sole rights to deliver babies in their household.

India's professions have always been interlinked with caste practices that dictated the professions of castes and its many subsets. Occupations were meant to be passed on from father to son, and the option of transitioning from one profession to another was generally outlawed. The Kayasth class, who comprised the upper layer of Hindu society, occupied high governmental positions, often serving as administrators or advisers. The lower classes such as the nais or the *chamar*s performed the menial jobs of barbers and tanners, respectively, while their wives doubled up as masseuses or pedicurists for the women of the aristocratic families. The *rudaali*s, or the professional mourners, whom I interviewed for this book are an example of caste-induced professions too. It is customary in Rajasthan for higher-caste women to not mourn publically, and so the rudaalis— mostly helpless, impoverished women caught in the web of caste hierarchy—step in to mourn on behalf of these upper-caste women, representing their sorrows for the traditional twelve-day mourning period. But the changing times, enculturation and automation are all slowly eliminating these mourning practices, consigning them as some sort of an anthropological curiosity. Increasingly, jobs are being taken up for monetary reasons, and technology is helping them switch quicker to economically viable jobs. No caste exists for a call-centre employee or a computer operator, for example.

To those who belong outside caste-bound practices—the calligraphers, the *kabootarbaaz*, the ittar wallahs—their professions have suffered because they lost their patrons in the kings, noblemen and moneyed zamindars of pre–Independence India. I must mention the incredible contribution of the Mughal empire, particularly Emperor Akbar. Almost five of the eleven professions I cover in this book gained prominence during the regime of the empire which was steeped in Parso-Arabic values along with Hindu influences.

Sometime during my travels I started working on this book, *The Lost Generation*. A few stories had taken me to the boondocks, far beyond the urban reaches of the states. I bumped into Naxalites, activists, thugs and ruffians, but rather than obstructing the story in any way, they helped me understand the complex social fabric of our vast country. To protect their identities and interests, in some cases I had to change their names or modify the factual matrix. Through our conversations, I saw that their paradoxes provided for a deeper understanding of issues rather than cause moral obstructions—all contributing to appreciating the frailty of the human condition. Like one of the readers of an early draft of this book said, 'There are hardly better ways to expose vulnerabilities and contradictions than reproducing the seemingly banal conversations about people's "ordinary lives".' In some instances, though, because of certain limitations faced by my translators and to best represent the views of the individuals, I have paraphrased conversations rather than document them verbatim. I have tried, then, to keep the stories free of authorial interference, something I have allowed to creep into the narrative only when necessary. Inescapably, however, I ended up directing the conversations to areas of my own interest, and I hope these areas interest you, the reader, as well.

While recording the interviews, I found myself being critical of the patriarchal, casteist, classist and sexist world-view seemingly espoused by these professions and the organized religion they practise. But at the same time I was grieving the loss of these ancient vocations, the cultural diversities and mysterious characters they have produced over the years. By the time I finished working on the book, I hoped to have arrived at a conclusion. I wish I could have assertively stated that these professions have been culturally exhausted, that they have lived out their natural lives, that they, then, have to go—that the world doesn't need the bhisti wallahs to exist if they have become an anachronism.

But then I don't make my living as a bhisti wallah.

1

THE GODNA ARTISTS
OF JHARKHAND

The Naxalites here in Jharkhand are formidable; they can hang you to death for beating up your wife in their kangaroo courts[1] or behead women for blackmailing men. In 2014, they bombed an empty school in a nearby village because they suspected the teachers of being informers to the police. The Naxals usually lurk in the shadows of the surrounding jungles like wildcats, preying on forest officers and moneyed travellers, and they recruit tribals living in hills and forests from the surrounding areas where people's lives are not important enough for the rest of the country to notice—enmeshed and embroiled in caste traditions and, most importantly, deprivation.

Salim, a local from Ranchi who has agreed to escort me through this Naxal-infested jungle, tells me all this in a low voice as we walk on the stony path. 'But they are tribal at heart—happy with a bottle of foreign liquor,' he adds. He stops as we jump over a rivulet with more mud in it than water. We have been walking for a while now through the thickets of Khunti district in Jharkhand, less formidable than some of its inhabitants. The early-morning views are idyllic—rolling hills, black, white and ochre cows grazing on the slopes, the occasional waterfall in the wildernesses—and make for an excellent picnic spot. There are rows and rows of palash trees on the horizon, lit up by the astounding eruptions of their beautiful orange-red flowers, like sparks raging from a forest fire beneath.

A tribal hamlet appears a few kilometres into the jungle, about thirty thatched huts scattered about like drunken men after a merry revelry. A gathering of women have formed a circle in a cleared patch of land, some with chubby babies hanging at their waists. Two musicians from the village—a drummer and a man plunking at a stringed instrument—sit in a corner outside the circle. There is a volley of hooting cries and then a rattle of drums, the soundtrack to which a mother from a nearby hut drags her squealing daughter by the arm. Thick tears of protest flow down the child's cheeks and on to her sleeveless frock as she is pulled to the middle of the circle.

'This is the child's *godna* ceremony,' Salim whispers as we watch from a distance. If a girl child is old enough to walk, she must be tattooed; the tattoo is known as 'godna'. Rarely is the ritual deferred until the early teens, and in any case it must be accomplished before the girl is married.

Tears drip down the face of the child, her shoulders shaking with quiet sobs as her mother whispers something in her ear—perhaps the promise of rice boiled in sweet milk to be prepared for her later in the evening. The mother rocks her rhythmically, soothing the harsh, painful thoughts in her daughter's head; perhaps she is hoping the next child she is carrying in her visibly pregnant belly is a son who can escape this pain.

The *malhar*,[2] or the tattoo artist—who will engrave the godna—pulls out the tools with his soot-covered hand. The crowd cheers as he picks up a three-pronged metal implement and meticulously begins to make a tilak on the child, Nekka's, forehead—a teardrop-shaped mark between her eyebrows. With each rap of the malhar's old instrument, droplets of blood begin to form around the lesions. They converge to form a stream of blood that spills down the child's cheek. A few women break into song and dance, a ritual, going round and round in circles, the child momentarily distracted by them.

> *Ningan koy Nekka pello kakro parmiya*
> *Ningan pelo ne chhorabao*
> *Ninghai joodi jonkhas koda raji keras,*
> *Ningan pelo ne chhorabao . . . Nekka*

> *The crab is nibbling on you dear girl, Nekka,*
> *Who will save you from it?*
> *Your boyfriend has left for foreign lands*
> *Who will save you from it?*

They sing obscene songs about loose pyjamas that falls off a man's smooth backside and then another about a cat chasing a dog up to the river, diverting the child's attention with the debauchery. The child cackles with laughter, even as tears hang precariously on her jaws, like dewdrops from a leaf.

A few more songs later, the singers plunge down on to the dust with arms stretched out, signifying the celebration of the girl's definite journey to heaven after death and her reunification with her ancestors. Just then, a needle slips and digs a bit too deep into the child's skin, pulling it upwards like an earthworm on a fishing hook, making the child scream in pain. The singers sit up, shaking their heads, disapproving of the child's weak will. An old lady— tall, lean and bent at the waist, with tattoo marks folding into a graceful network of fine wrinkles along her neck and face—jumps up and the drummer steps up the rhythm in anticipation.

'The road to the Lord is full of obstacles,' she addresses the audience in Kurukh, a Dravidian language. 'The door is guarded heavily by large, black demons,' the old one narrates, clawing her fingers and sticking her tongue out to signify the demon. The child quietens down, drawing images of the dark, the perilous dungeon of the Lord, in her head. 'Those without the godna,' the old lady roars, 'will be branded with hot coals in hell, thrown on cacti and pushed through sugarcane extracting machines.'

This purgatory has been described to the child before, in the old folk tales and legends of the evil men who steal sweets from the village kitchens. The child sits quietly through the rest of the ceremony, wincing every now and then, as if wondering which woman in the crowd looked most like the demon that was just described. The rest of the ceremony is carried out on the instructions of the old lady, Nowri Tikri, who turns out to be the child's grandmother. There is more song and dance, and bananas from a wild tree nearby and tea are passed around to the assembly of about fifteen people.

It is afternoon by the time the malhar finishes tattooing the child's forehead, and even cheeks—on the insistence of the grandmother—to prevent evil spirits from casting their eyes on the child. The tattoos look more like angry, swollen welts than works of art; it will be another few weeks before they become dark, pigmented symbols in the shape of fat-bellied raindrops, symbols to promote safe delivery during childbirth. The musicians and dancers have long retired to their fields, and the child is tired—dried blood congealed on her cheeks and eyes drooping with sleep. But she has to be washed, according to the grandmother, before being taken back inside her hut. 'The malhar is from a lower caste,' Nowri tells us as we arch closer. She bends over the child, closely monitoring the mother as she smears turmeric paste all over the child's body.

'Careful, now! Use the turmeric sparingly,' Nowri spits, baring her remaining teeth. 'My son works hard for this money!'

The touch of the lower-caste malhar on the child is believed to have caused contamination and requires a purging of the dirt with warm water and haldi. Nowri reminisces that as a young girl, when malhars came to the village for godna, they would use the route along the village that passed through the jungles. These untouchable men were not allowed footwear once inside the village and were barred from wearing clothes above the waist and below the knees, even in the cold winters of the forests. In those days, if the malhar or their womenfolk, known as *malaharin*, were given food for their services, the bowl which they had touched would be cleaned with cow urine (which was considered auspicious) and then heated over fire to be purified.

Nowri herself had never allowed a malhar into the house for each of her three daughters' godnas. 'We still don't,' she says assertively, slapping on some fresh gobar—a natural cooling agent as well as an antiseptic—on to the child's wounds to prevent infection. Her thick silver bangles clang together like ancient temple bells, louder than the soft, clinking sounds made by the shiny glass bangles her daughter-in-law wears. Beneath the silver bangles, one can see the faded green marks of a tattoo all the way up her elbow.

'The ladies of the village envied my godna. I would sit still like a statue whenever I got them done. The more godna you get done, the stronger you become—both in terms of spirit and physical prowess,' Nowri explains. 'Children are weak these days. I got an entire arm done by a malhar when I was all of eleven years old. But Nekka's godna will be split over the years till she gets married,' she speaks of the child. 'When the God of Death, Yamraj, approaches her during her time of death, he will immediately identify her and not confuse her with her husband. In a way, Nekka gets these tattoos to protect her husband from Yamraj. A year later, we can get one done on her back, then another on her neck and some on her arms,' she mutters, slapping another layer of fresh green gobar on to the now-sleeping child, her head resting on her mother's lap.

'More tattoos?' I ask.

'Yes.'

'Why?'

'These are our ornaments, our assets. The only things we take with us to the heavens.' Nowri smoothens the wrinkles on her hand, revealing a complex pattern of dots and lines, like binary codes, engraved on her hand; an octagon with a dot in the middle near her elbow is a lotus—the pedestal of Goddess Lakshmi, the distributor of wealth; triangles along her upper arm represent Yoni—the goddess of femininity or womanly strength, translating literally to vagina or womb; and a set of concentric circles down to her wrist represent the nine planets that control the destinies of the wearer.

Godna finds its roots in ancient India, in pieces of history documenting life and culture along this side of the subcontinent. While citations refer to it all the way back to the fifteenth century, it is hard to determine its exact antiquity. Around the sixteenth century, Tavernier, a French traveller and jewel merchant,[3] wrote in an article that the women of Banjera (East Bengal) tattooed their skin from the waist upwards. These nomadic communities did this as a mark of identity as they wandered from place to place. One clue regarding godna's antiquity may be found in comparing petroglyph designs of labyrinths dating back to 2500 BC on a riverbank at Pansaimol,[4] Goa, that have similar designs as those of a godna—but of course this might only be mere speculation. But the only accessible and available historical records we have are the oral narratives of women like Nowri Tikri, narrating the tales of their own grandmothers' who patterned their body with a variety of symmetrical tattoos in indigo.

'It has healing properties too. Look at this,' Nowri says, pointing to a dark mole-like tattoo on her throat. 'I got it done a couple of years back to cure my goitre. It disappeared for a few years,' she says, snapping her fingers, perhaps hinting at the acupuncture effects that godna is rumoured to have, 'but then it came back . . . Pakhi, the village medic, suggested eating a medicine made of pig's throat, and Durki, the old witch whom villagers prayed to, made me stand on my head every day for hours,' she scowls. 'But nothing worked. It is the work of evil spirits, that is it . . .' She pauses, her face contorting into a frown as she spots something, pursing her lips and distending her nostrils—a grimace that her daughter-in-law immediately appears to recognize as threatening, for she holds the child closer.

'*Ai* you,' she screams at the malhar, hobbling rheumatically towards him. He is washing his face at a well near her dwelling. 'Do not go near my well,' she screams, hurling a few Kurukh[5] curses at him. With a hand covering his mouth, making an irrefutably urgent excuse and offering an unspecific apology, the malhar scuttles away.

'Defiling the water in my well, that mouse . . .' Nowri mutters under her breath.

'Does he live here?' I ask her.

'No, no, they have no homes. They are nomads.'

'So how did you catch a hold of him for the godna ceremony?'

'They travel from village to village performing godna and making copper utensils in their free time. My brother told me that he had spotted this malhar, Dubru, near the village. He saw him while coming from the fields and summoned him immediately. We give them a bag of rice or a few coins in exchange. Dubru will stay here in the shed for a night and leave tomorrow morning. Unfortunately, the shed is near my well. I hope the midget doesn't defile my well. Oh, it'll be the curse of the Gods if it happens . . .' she says, disappearing into her hut, murmuring a curse about constipation plaguing him for the rest of his life.

Malhars are the male members of the Hindu coppersmith caste. Heinz-Jürgen Pinnow, a German scholar,[6] mentions in his book that this caste is considered especially dirty and lazy and that the name is often used as an insult. Malhars do not farm or sell wares. They do not go to schools. They have no addresses, nor any official papers. They have no representative in the government or panchayat that they can look to for help or lodge complaints with, nor do they have any expectations from the government. They look for a place in the fringes of the villages—under trees, haystacks, some barren land usually labelled by the village panchayats as useless. Malhars move around with their wives and children—and with bare possessions—much like the nomads in an African slum described by the Polish author Ryszard Kapuściński in his article 'City of Nomads': 'Many of my neighbors here have just the one thing. Someone has a shirt, someone a *panga*, someone a pickaxe. The one with a shirt can find a job as a night watchman (no one wants a half-naked guard); the one with a panga can be hired to cut down weeds; the one with the pickaxe can dig a ditch. Others have only their muscles to sell.'

Dubru, although a malhar, is privileged because he owns two things—a prong and a shirt. What he lacks is muscle. Dubru is puny, with the thin skin around his mouth shrivelling like that of an old prune. He sits under the shed, thatched with dried hay, lazily scratching his stomach and buttocks, yawning as he makes lampblack. A small cup-shaped oil lamp made of baked clay has a wick burning placed near him. A few inches above is another lamp, inverted, collecting the soot from the burning lamp. 'We mix this with a mother's milk to make the tattoo ink,' he says in a croaky voice that is somewhere between a whimper and a song as I sit beside him. The air fills with the smell of alcohol apparent on his breath and through a discarded plastic Sprite bottle with apple-juice-coloured liquid. Dubru often uses this *handiya*, a rice wine, instead of water—even to clean his mouth in the morning. Light filters through the bottle and a green reflection flickers on his shirt that is stained with the little vignettes of his life—soot, dust, turmeric and handiya.

Every morning at sunrise, Dubru travels many kilometres from village to village on his slippers that have lost all their tread, through paths in this rainforest that are strewn with dried leaves, traversing shady paths that move with the sun. On most days, he starts his morning with leftover rice that charitable villagers give away to nomads like him. On some good days, he may have performed a godna or carved out a vessel, which can possibly fetch him tea or even a boiled egg from the money made. But he definitely prefers handiya over tea. Half a pint of this stuff is sufficient; it not only makes him forget hunger but also provides nourishment— for the soul, at least. As dawn arrives with a fanfare of singing koels, he is often spotted by passers-by passed out in what can roughly be called happiness.

'Before I drew blood,' Dubru says—talking carefully to avoid a slur, but his moustache becoming a hindrance; the thin hair curling into his mouth in the absence of substantial lips—'I whispered prayers under my breath to the spirits in the trees. I avoided handiya because the ill spirits might be put off by them and cause pain to the child or curse me with a lifelong illness,' he says, twisting his moustache. 'Of course, you can smoke though,' he adds quickly as I eye the beedi stubs in one corner of the hut. 'And if you or I or the child had interrupted the ritual by running away, this would have been a very bad omen and I would have had to stop right away. The child's family would then have had to perform prayers for the spirits.' He shakes his head. According to him, the dark spirits do not wish for the tattooing to continue then and it has to be postponed till the next day.

'Godna is a highly regarded and carefully followed ritual here,' he continues, mumbling. 'Lactating mothers rarely want to donate their milk these days. Their milk is said to be the purest and closest to the composition of human blood,' he says, clicking his tongue in disapproval, picking at the soot ingrained in his nails. 'Till a few years back, it was a noble deed, an act that would make the Gods happy. But they want to keep it only for their babies these days. So I mix cow's milk sometimes.'

The spirits expect Dubru to act suitably. If he doesn't, they'll inflict death and destruction upon him and his subjects.

'Has anyone ever been infected after the Godna?' I ask him.

'*Ihi thatha amba nana* [Do not joke]. No one has ever fallen ill after I made the godna. In other places, they have to stuff the girl's mouth with a cloth in case she bites her tongue in pain. But I don't need that. I have the blessings of my ancestors. The chants help, and I very carefully indent the upper layer of the skin. It requires skill and craft,' he smiles, proudly, looking at his plastic bottle, as if it had the spirits perched atop it, rewarding Dubru for every godna he performs.

He takes a swig from it, a few drops dripping down his arm, which has a sleeve full of godna. 'These I inscribed myself when I had leftover soot and ink,' he says with a burp. 'Men hardly get these tattoos around here, but the Oraons[7] sometimes burn the skin of boys with a lighted stick to mark their coming of age.[8] They move into that *dumkuria*,' he says, pointing to a shed which is a meeting place for the men of the community in this village, 'where older boys mark the younger ones. But some may simply do it for ornamentation. Look at this godna, there is *jawaphool*, the young sprout of wheat,' he explains, pointing to a five-sided leafy figure on his bony chest.

'This other one, though, I regret. It was unlucky for me,' he says, pointing to a tattoo near his wrist known as the Kanhaiya's *mukut*—Krishna with his beloved wife, Rukmini. 'My wife happened to leave me for heaven right after I got this. The godna though ensures that her memory remains, even as it fades away.'

A few years ago Dubru married a girl. They travelled together in groups, like malhars did. But she had cholera and no government hospital would admit them because of the absence of residential proof. 'How would we have a fixed residence?' he says, nodding his head as he narrates the story. 'This is how we have always lived. When someone is tired of travelling, they erect a shack. Some other malhars put up another one beside it. And then another. And if we fall short of water and food in that area, we just abandon these homes and move somewhere else,' Dubru says, shrugging his shoulders. 'So she died.'

'Nobody taught me this craft,' Dubru says, sighing, as he collects the soot in the centre of the earthen lamp. 'I just saw my parents practise it on the villagers. They also made utensils—both earthen and metal—on fires. My mother helped me make these prongs, my very own pair with a bamboo stick and thorns from shrubs. My parents can't travel any more so I left them behind a few years ago. We are the eternal nomads. It turns out that except these permanent marks of godna everything in our life is temporary,' he says, laughing. Even parents.

I ask him what will he do when he gets old? He looks at me quizzically. 'I'll also live in a village and die. After one last sip of handiya.' He laughs. 'Anyway, that time is near. I might also live on roots and rats like old men and women in villages do. Except for these Naxal parties who want to flaunt their tribal legacy for political interests, nobody wants a godna anymore,' he says.

Tribal students also tend to avoid godna or get them removed at tattoo-removal clinics, due to bullying by urban students or other reasons. Many tribal women also get married to men in villages and cities now, their sensibilities having been altered by years of urban upbringing. The men prefer not to be spotted with wives sporting traditional godna and often leave them behind at homes for social assemblies.

'But never mind,' Dubru whimpers, looking at the now-finished bottle of handiya. 'The rest of us will keep our fading, spreading tattoos, the few links between our past and present.'

2

THE RUDAALIS OF RAJASTHAN

A thin layer of desert sand has enveloped everything by the time I wake up on the upper bunk of the overnight train—my mouth, the Ondaatje book which I use as a bolster for my head and my leaking thermos of water.

The sand reappears almost as soon as I dust it off, flying in from the open windows as the train skirts a last long stretch of desert before coming to a clanking stop at the Jaisalmer station, among crackling oil lanterns on hawkers' carts and the yammer of red-coated coolies making their way through the multitude with suitcases jammed on their heads.

Outside the station, I scour the parking area for Satar Khan, my driver for the journey, whom I find waiting outside his jeep, holding a placard with my name spelt wrong. He nods at me, taking my bag quietly, and starts the incapacitated engine. It is an hour before dawn. From my last few visits here I know that in some time the peacocks will perch on the khejri trees and pick on the unripe sangria, women will appear on the horizon with shimmering brass pots on their heads. But there is still time before the sun rises as we wade through the twilight into the rolling dunes, leaving the highways behind, the sand grains climbing into the car like a sinking ship filling with water.

19

Twice we get lost under these remaining stars of the night. Satar then stops his vehicle, flashes his torch, and looks for a path in the ever-changing dunes—perhaps looking for a jeep trail or the direction of the wind. And then he speeds back down the dunes, finding the North Star that will guide us out of here.

Satar is a tall, burly man who looks like he has spent his life in the grey safari suit he is wearing at the moment; rich white strands peek through the cover of his oiled black hair, his light hazel eyes, prematurely wrinkled, seem to say he has all the time in the sun.

'Are you sure about going to this village?' he suddenly asks me as we drive through the dunes, turning his head to me, his long neck punctuated by a protruding Adam's apple. 'Even the police think twice before going there. Just be careful, okay,' he whispers when I nod. 'They don't like being photographed by straying tourists and the like,' he adds. I tuck my camel-sized camera beneath the seat.

'Driving through the dunes is like an ant walking on a rug,' he says looking out of the rolled-down window, as the first light of dawn breaks through the sky. A vacant desert horizon looms before us, and except for an occasional camel tinkling by with *ghungroo*s tied to its hooves, the earth looks as if its skin has been peeled away—without the greenery, animals and people to clothe it. Nothing is permanent in this desert which moves like a wild sea, the landscape altering each time a breeze whispers or a sandstorm roars by—taking, moving, shifting things. But rocks, camel tracks, and passages of an ancient river,[1] rumoured to have disappeared below the earth—civilizations as old as time itself—still exist, magical survivors of the past.

For a while, there is nothing much to see except the changing light and, then, *dhanis*, or clusters of mud huts start sprouting on either side of the road, like discarded toys amongst rocks. Satar slows down after crossing a signboard in Hindi with the name of the village, steering the jeep on to another road for a few kilometres and then finally continuing up a drive to stop at a herd of cows that are tied to a pole.

'That's the village you were talking about,' he mutters, halting the car at the edge of the road.

A few mud houses seem to surround a large pukka haveli that's been standing here for years, sand collecting in its grooves and niches. The village has a population of 1200,[2] but apart from a turbaned old man smoking a beedi under a tree and two horses grazing on dried hay, there is not a soul in sight—unlike other dhanis which are the centres of activity during early mornings. This hamlet, 23 kilometres from the princely town of Jaisalmer, is among the seven or eight regions still under the fierce control of the kith and kin of the Rajputs, with its multitude of cobblers, chickpea farmers, blacksmiths, Brahmins, and so on. Everyone is supposed to be completely content to be performing their prearranged—inherited—roles. There is no police station or school in the village; the nearest school is a government-run institution comprising about twenty-three students about 10 kilometres away. This nowhere place lies outside the larger economics of a country, and the presence of the state, if at all, is feeble and personified in the form of the thakur of the area.

'I think the Thakur has instructed them to be in their homes,' whispers Satar, fidgeting with the key ring of the car. 'Told you, they don't like visitors. They do this every time a cop or local MLA or stray foreigner drops in.' Warily, I dial the Thakur's mobile-phone number.

'Haloooo?' says the Thakur, in a thick raspy voice, as if his words were pressed between sandpaper before being spoken aloud.

'Yes, come, come. Walk up towards the haveli. I have been waiting for you,' he says, ending the call.

'Thakurs can be daunting because they are connected to the royal families which apparently still exert considerable influence in the Marwar and Jaisalmer regions in Rajasthan,' Satar explains to me as we walk up a dusty path. 'They also have licensed guns which they use for hunting purposes. This thakur is a Rawat Rajput,[3] a very high caste, and he wants his formidable image to be retained. *Mein bhi khud darta hun inse*. [I myself am scared of them.]'

The Thakur sits on a charpoy outside his whitewashed haveli, wearing a stark white dhoti-kurta; a thick gold chain with a Hanuman pendant disappears between the buffalo humps around his neck. I scan the haveli behind him. A veiled woman peeps out from a *jharokha* on the upper floor of the building. She quickly disappears when she catches me looking.

The feudal lord's progeny still carries his weight in the environs of the village. Eight or nine men called *chela*s, or followers, surround him—two attending to his horse cart, others sitting like hens on their eggs, by his feet, and the rest standing with their hands behind their backs, trotting around him in circles. In reality as well as in the pages of history these sidekick roles are demarcated as efficiently and clearly as that of a ship steward's. These chelas are actually *daroga*s,[4] the hereditary servants who are the illegitimate offspring of a thakur with a *daori*,[5] or female servant. The girls who were born to daoris were mostly killed at birth; the rest were either given away as dowry during the weddings of their legitimate daughters to chiefs and nobles, or married to other chelas.

The nobles, chiefs and thakurs housed the daoris in separate accommodations, often on the fringes of the havelis. Apart from serving as concubines for these thakurs, the daoris also doubled as *rudaali*s, or mourners, for the family in times of death and sickness.

'Do you know His Highness of Jodhpur? Yes, the maharaja and I are descendants of the same family,' the Thakur announces proudly. 'I also recently attended a wedding in the Jaisalmer maharaja's family. Madam, we are warm and hospitable to our worst enemies too, unlike people in your cities, *hai na*, Satar?' he said, turning to look at my driver, who is squatting with the Thakur's other servants. 'I have seen you around. Wasn't your father a *khaas* [special] chela of my father . . . Ah, anyway, we'll talk later,' he tells Satar, as his other servants move their head in accord. By now, Satar has folded both his hands and is nodding fervently. The Thakur would be able to peddle him for a few bags of grain, for nothing.

'So what is it that you want to know, madam?'

'Do you have rudaalis here?'

'Yes, they live here. They rise early in the morning, finish their work and help around the village. This village mostly has my family members. Like branches of this big khejri tree . . . spread all over. So if someone dies, she visits them and shares their sorrows with them.' His thick features are at once simple and extravagant. His eyes are small, so small and deep that it's tough to look into them directly.

'Someone has to cry when the members of our royal families die, right?' he says, the tone calculating, controlled and formal; his eyes never sit on one person but glide through his audience listening to the monologue; he asks questions but does not wait for replies.

'Women's brains are hardwired to feel loss and grief. They have a weak heart,' the Thakur says, patting his chest under his kurta. 'We don't allow the women in our families to make a sight of themselves outside our homes. High-caste woman do not cry in front of commoners. Even if their husbands die, they need to preserve their dignity. These low-caste women, rudaalis, do the job for them. The whole village feels the loss . . . She represents their sadness,' he says, concluding his speech, and the chelas furiously nod their heads, as if mentally applauding him.

'Do they live with their families or—'

'No, no,' interjects the Thakur before I can finish the question. 'They live in their own *kutiya* near the haveli. These women have no family. We are their family. The whole village is their family. Once they leave their home and come as a gift to me in marriage, they never go back, even to visit. They have to live with us in the village and serve us menfolk. *Achha . . . aur batao*, what else do you want to talk about?' he grunts, getting restless.

'Can I meet them?'

'No, madam, our women have to preserve their *lajja*,' he answers immediately, as if the possibility of such a feat had never been considered before. 'They can't be out in the open. It is their duty to take care of the children and men of the households. We don't allow them to meet strangers. After all, we have to protect their virtue. You can ask me whatever you want to know. They are delicate fragile things . . .' He raises his hands, as if trying to catch an elusive half-moon. 'My father used to tell me that we really need to look after them. Most women in the zenana are busy right now. My newborn son keeps them occupied,' he says, laughing uproariously, taking pride in having fathered a sixth son.

Obliging my request to walk around the village, the Thakur sends one of his chelas (or the daroga) with me and Satar, instructing him to walk with a thick lathi in his hand. And when I dismiss the need for them to do so, the Thakur laughs. 'Just in case you come across miscreants and stray dogs,' he offers, his paws on his paunch.

The chela walks behind us, his eyes lowered, fixed on the path ahead of us. Young boys warily trickle out of their homes and hunt for their green marbles in the hot sand. A middle-aged woman cleaning her pots with sand, covered head to toe in a black translucent *odhni* over a tight-fitting mirrored backless choli, runs back into her home when she sees us, peeping out of the half-closed door.

'Do you have any sisters?' I ask the chela, a young boy with lost brown eyes.

'No, two were born to my mother, but died a few days after they were born. We don't keep girl children, madam.'

Pushing the envelope a bit further, I ask one of the boys, 'So is the Thakur your father?'

'No, madam, I only have a mother. We are not supposed to have fathers. My mother also never had a father,' he replies, in a low, even tone, his head slightly lowered. 'That's my mother,' he says, glancing at another veiled woman peeping through the door. She lifts a shoulder in acknowledgement. I wish I could see her eyes—to check if they tell a story.

By now, the pitiless sun is reflected off the burning sand. We approach the gentle slope of a sand hill. At its peak, a crowning silhouette appears on a far-off set of hills—the centuries-old fortress of Sonar Kila in the city of Jaisalmer, with its great walls and crenelated towers set against a vast, empty sky, a well-girded medieval town within it that is untouched by time, still retaining age-old legends, stories and, along with them, archaic rituals.

Satar informs me as we drive out of the village that the daoris are the mistresses of these Thakurs, and that if they reproduce with them, the children never have an official father. 'Their ration cards, voter IDs, all have names only of the mothers, who retain their maiden name as their surname, but sometimes they don't even have that. If a daori has to be taken to the hospital for childbirth—which rarely happens because midwives deliver the babies at home—it's in a fully packed car. No one is allowed to see her during all of those nine months. If a girl is born, she is mostly "laid to rest" right away. The birth of a daughter, even from a legitimate wife, is not liked by the Rajputs. It is felt that the father of a girl is would automatically have to show himself as inferior at the time of her marriage,' he says.

'Inferior?' I croak.

'Do you know what the going rate for dowry[6] is around here, madam?' he says in a mocking tone.

'It is six to eight kilos of gold at least. Plus, if you are from a rich family, you have to give them servants, cars, silver, welcome them with your heads lowered, and heed to their incessant demands. Last year, a girl's wedding took place for the first time in this village in eighty years. She was among the few who survived. They tried to poison her but she vomited it out. So her family assumed that she was a gift from Lord Krishna and kept her.'

'Do they not protest, Satar, these biological sons of the Thakur and these rudaalis?'

'It's rare, madam. Most villagers are not educated. They are really supressed and aren't allowed to flourish. It's a caste-bound community. The lower castes will always remain only lower castes. Rudaalis here belong to the Darogi community and, in a way, have better lives than the rudaalis who live in the villages independently, like those of Mirasi community,[7] who do not serve the thakurs. At least the Thakur looks after the Darogis financially. The others have to fend for themselves.

Satar asks me if I have heard the popular rudaali saying that goes:

Pando bhalo na kosko, beti bhali naek

Leno bhalo na baapko, sahib rakhya tek.

[Walking on foot even for a mile is not favoured, nor is the birth of a single daughter.

A debt of one's father is not favoured, so may God protect us from these misfortunes.]

By being concubines, rudaalis from the Darogi community have access to their feudal lords and their families, and would never otherwise be acknowledged as legitimate consorts. Where women's participation in the public realm is carefully policed, occupying the position of a concubine gives them and their children access to the homes of rich landed men. They pray—to the god Bheruji,[8] who himself was a lusty bachelor and loved seducing young girls, especially from lower castes—for these men to live long lives. In a way, they seize these cultural and religious practices to achieve dignity, which—otherwise, being landless, impoverished women—would not be accessible to them.

The Rajputs have always been wistful of their past and keenly conscious of their genealogy, Satar explains to me. They emphasized a Rajput ethos that was martial in spirit, with a fierce pride in lineage and tradition. They claimed prerogatives and privileges over the general population and were eager to maintain them. They also devised rituals where their high status and position was preserved, which translated into elaborate death rituals. Lamenters and mourners, hence, gained precedence, and unfortunate women who were widowed, impoverished or served as servants in the royal households were turned into rudaalis, or professional mourners. 'The rudaali, somewhat "chose" her future the moment she survived her birth to a lower-caste mother,' murmurs Satar.

***

We get back on to the roads by afternoon, crossing alternate acres of rocky and sandy ground. The delicate violet flowers of the aak tree, the yellow crispiness of the jharberis, the white whiskers of the snowbush—all the seeds of these deserts lie dormant, soundless, sightless, unawake; wait they must for the weather to change, for the old to be replaced by the new. The dunes are lit a bright orange by now, undulating ridges set by hot winds, and criss-crossed by the large tracks of desert jeeps, a few camel trails and the smaller, stranger ones of a scorpion trudging across the sand.

A young man from the Meena community is almost at his deathbed in a nearby village, the Thakurs chela had informed us. 'The Meena is an upper-caste community. The rudaalis have already assembled outside his home. The village isn't far, about six kilometres from here,' he'd said, pointing southwards. We drive into the quiet village with a few mud and straw homes in sight, all scattered across the yellowed terrain. Most of the huts face away from the wind blowing in from the deserts, each of them closed within a mud wall which is short and pocked with holes. Parched khejri trees and bare methi jhaar offer feeble relief from the sun with their scanty shade. Barefoot children play on the street, rolling a mud ball with a stick. They stop skipping around when they see us and watch us curiously as we come to a halt.

'Have you come for Kundan Kakosa?' inquires one of them, coming forward. 'Go there.' He points his stick in the direction of a two-storeyed pukka house, but follows us nevertheless, guiding us around his village. It is the only pukka house in the village, outside which a small group of people have gathered. Among the party are several men whose white cotton dhotis are fluttering in the hot wind. There is a cripple who usually begs outside the village temple, manoeuvring himself on his hands, hoping to procure some alms from the gathering. The sarpanch is a square-shouldered man whose expression speaks of restlessness. He is inquiring into Kundan's farmlands and asking after the deceased's inebriated son who was being given glasses of lemon water to rid him of his hangover so as to make him able enough to perform his father's last rites. The women squat separately on the ground.

Three rudaalis stand out among the crowd, dressed in black odhnis while the rest of the women sit with their long, colourful veils drawn down to their chins. They all look into the hut where Kundan has been placed on a bed of sacred kusa grass, on a spot circled by cow dung.

A few male relatives hover above Kundan while a pandit places a sprig of tulsi and pours a few drops of water from the Ganga river into his mouth to delay the messengers of Yama, the god of death. A cow is brought to stand next to him and then hurriedly pushed out moments later into the backyard through another door. Kundan was supposed to grasp the cow's tail to signify his safe carriage to the other world but before he could do so, he took his last breath. A relative feels his pulse and silently declares him dead. And the rudaalis immediately break into action.

They gasp and cry loudly, tossing their heads back, and wail to the heavens, beating their chests and slapping the ground in front of them. Their veils drop every now and then, exposing their faces and long necks tattooed with traditional symbols. Soon, thick tears start flowing, staining their cheeks with black kohl in the process, falling on to their odhnis. They don't wipe the tears away, most dry under the hot sun before fresh ones flow down.

This upper-caste funeral procession is a performance—with the village as its audience—of pomp and pageantry. Once the villagers have all assembled, they trudge up to the widow sitting behind a veil, her shoulders shaking with silent sobs, to break her glass bangles by banging them together and remove the red kumkum in her *maang*,[9] thus solemnizing her move into widowhood.

'*Arrey, tharo toh suhag giyore* [Oh, your husband is now dead],' they cry, holding the widow's hands. '*Arrey ab tharo ei duniya mein kain wajood re* [What is the reason for your existence in this world now],' they beat their chests. The pandit starts his chants along with two of his assistants. He usually sends a subordinate to perform the rites, but Kundan was a known landlord and fed the Brahmins every Saturday, and that demanded the pandit's presence.

'*Aum Namo Narayana, Aum Nama Sivaya,*' they chant. The pandit pulls out a small jar with sandalwood paste and applies it on the dead man's forehead. A lamp is lit near his head and incense is burned while the pandit reads out more chants from his booklet.

Every time a visitor enters, the rudaalis wail louder in a show of irreplaceable grief and loss. Then, in one of the most striking features of their enactment, the women move their torsos together in circles, beating their chests in a cadence. '*Hey ram, hey ram,*' they chant. But the audience watches them, falling into the trance weaved by them, giving into their grief, letting their eyes well up looking at the sight.

Some touch the feet of the deceased Kundan, some hover about for a few minutes and, having seen to the formalities and having asked the polite questions, settle into a silence and eventually leave. The rest sing praises in his memory.

'Yes, yes, he liked his moustache trimmed downwards,' says his barber.

'He helped me get my daughter married to his munshi's son. What a great man!' whispers another.

'He did that without any commission?' asks another.

'Just two kilos of gold and my three goats.'

Intervals between the crying and mourning sessions only come when the rudaalis break for lunch, provided by the relatives of the deceased—some leftover rotis from the morning and raw onions. The role of the aristocratic women, meanwhile, is restricted to within the grieving house, where, after the body leaves the home, private rituals continue. But this is only the first session: the performance goes on for twelve days after a death. A longer mourning period better explains the family's class denomination, and the more theatrical the act, the more it is spoken about in the neighbours' homes.

'As long as a woman has a husband, she has esteem in the village,' says Feroja, one of the three rudaalis at the mourning. 'With him gone, she has to cover her face from strangers, keep away from pujas and be the unlucky one who caused her husband's death.'

We saunter back to the home of Feroja and Madami— her husband's brother's wife. They live together with Feroja's thirteen-year-old son, Bakoo. Both Feroja's and Madami's spouses died young in the same year due to an unexplained disease. Feroja lifts her veil as we walk an isolated path to her home. She looks to be in her early thirties—a worn woman, her fingers like twines, her feet cracked and hard—feet that have walked hundreds of miles through the desert to visit nearby villages for funerals. I suppose the old refugees travelling through borders must have looked much like Feroja.

These women took to becoming rudaalis about twelve years ago. Before that they travelled with their husbands, singing around the region for alms. 'We sang our way all over the desert. We sang about the river, the trees and sand dunes. We hunted in the desert, ate what we hunted and went from village to village. Wherever we went, we left a trail of music in our wake,' Feroja says wistfully, spinning her fingers around her head, virtually wrapping the whole world in a web of songs. 'And at last I think they felt exhausted. Both were young but they died the same year. We became signs of ill omen everywhere we went after that. Two widows whose ill luck killed their husbands. So we finally came back to our village and Bharauni bai introduced us to this work. She gave us her old black odhnis. Black symbolizes death. The favourite colour of the god of death, Yama,' she adds, tucking her odhni between her teeth to stop it from sliding off her head. 'Even Bharauni bai is dead now. Everyone dies. We knew we'd always get work in this profession.' The rest of the time, they live more or less conventional lives: help the villagers with odd chores such as making cow-dung cakes for lighting kitchen fires, chopping wood and cleaning homes.

The chorus of peacocks that had earlier filled the village had ceased and been replaced by the sound of the night insects, a steady humming background. A breeze is coming up. All the dogs in the village bark and then fall silent.

Feroja and Madami's home is a one-room tenement, a few minutes from the stone miners' homes where our car is parked. Large chunks of rocks lie around her hut. 'One day, my son will grow up and make pukka walls with cow dung, mud and straw.' They had recently acquired a *chakki*, which she shows us proudly. 'Before this, we had to buy ground wheat for rotis. It was expensive. Now we just buy the grains. We also grind wheat for our neighbours,' she says. 'They give us four rupees for five kilos of wheat.'

'How much do you earn from mourning for a death?' I ask her as she lights a fire while Madami flattens out the dough between her palms to make rotis.

'When we mourn at landlords' homes, they give us two hundred rupees for twelve days. But money is given only when rich people die. The rest just give us some coins. Sometimes, they give us only food—oil, *atta*, a bag of onions. Old odhnis and cholis too. For children's deaths, we don't charge anything. Sometimes, I wish they gave us milk or buttermilk. My son has never tasted milk,' Feroja laments. 'Oh, actually there was this one time when a far-off neighbour's goat wandered to our home. We milked her and had three glasses of milk that day,' she says, giggling, her face lighting up for a few moments.

'Did someone teach you how to cry for the mourning?'

'Nobody taught us,' chimes in Madami, a few years older than Feroja. 'We tell the widow stories of her husband, his smile and his eyes. We bring her sorrow to the surface, relieving her heart for a few hours at least.'

And she speaks from experience. Ten years ago, soon after their husbands died, Madami lost her fifteen-year-old son to dehydration, and his sister soon followed suit. She died at eighteen.

A heavy oil lamp hanging from the entrance is the only source of light for the women, casting great wondrous shadows on the walls. With every gust of wind that blows into the hut, bouquets of light and people are displaced in the room.

'Sometimes I think of my children when I want to cry and other times of my husband. He was a wretched man and slept around with *randi*s. But at least he gave me respect in society,' Madami says, her voice hoarse from all the wailing earlier in the day.

'And when we can't cry, we use the bark of aak leaves. They can make your eyes burn and water enough to make an oasis in the *registan*' she croaks, pulling out a small jar of aak which she keeps in a fabric purse stitched to the inseam of her ghaghra. 'We used to cry for a lot more days until a few years ago. Relatives who received the information via post arrived late and we were summoned to cry for them. But these days, mobile phones have taken over and messages are delivered instantly. So the mourning period is just twelve days. There are fewer rudaalis too. They exist only here in the villages in Marwar. The rest of them want more sophistication. Quiet funerals . . .' Madami says, her voice trailing away.

'People die a lot less often, too, these days,' adds Feroja, clicking her tongue, peeling the onion, but her eyes remain dry. 'They have started calling musicians these days, from Jaisalmer, for the mourning. I heard about it from a randi who came from the next village,' she tells Madami, who clucks her tongue in disapproval too. 'They can never console people like us. You need to feel things in here,' she says, placing a hand on her heart.

Aren't they worried that they will be displaced by these contemporary practices?

'Why, no, not at all. These singers can't fill their eyes and make tears well enough, can they?' Feroja says, fixing a plate for her son with a thick, dry roti, two raw onions and some salt. She calls out to him, *'Aye Bakoodaa.'* He comes running in, ravenously attacking his plate of food.

'There are only fifteen or twenty deaths in this village of eight hundred people. So many doctors come from cities nowadays . . . Also, we can no longer go to other villages. We don't understand the desert as well,' Feroja says with a weary grimace.

'Bharauni bai could,' she adds after pause. 'One must forever be learning, picking up signs and watching the clouds in the day and the stars in the night, the trail left by a *bichhoo* or the dacoits. To tell where she is, where others are, which tree is good to sleep under in the night, and which one has poisonous air . . .'

3

THE GENEALOGISTS
OF HARIDWAR

The labyrinth of winding streets and alleyways stretches into long, bustling markets, each side flanked by vendors who sell all kinds of wares—from locks and bus tickets to bhajan books and trinkets. Packed in between are sweet-lassi shops, dinky, box-shaped occurrences amongst hundreds of similar-looking spaces on both sides of the busy road that leads to the ghats—all perched on columns a few feet above their own putrid garbage. A rat surprises me by its sudden appearance; but it seems annoyed as well, flashing me a proprietorial scowl and then scuttling away before getting stamped flat by a swarm of humanity busily making its way to the temples, pandits and ghats.

Facing the long expanse of these streets, one thinks about the brevity of life, where even death becomes a commodity to be produced and reproduced for sale by its tradesmen—flower sellers, wood sellers trading wood for cremations, pandits, barbers, Aghoris, Mahapatras and the boatmen who carry the corpses.

An anxious-looking couple scan the street for a familiar landmark, searching for someone who can guide them out of here, perhaps wondering, Where have we arrived?—an inquiry that may pertain to his surroundings but becomes an experiential one.

We are in Haridwar—one of the holiest places in the world for Hindus—which, in one guise, is a kind of magnificent crematorium and, in other ways, is the address for temples, influential gurus and millions of their followers. And through this home of the divine and the dead flows the Ganges with its long stretches of smooth banks, one among seven[1] of the most revered locations in Hinduism, where one can attain moksha after death.

At the break of dawn Hindus throng the riverside, their bare feet planted on the soaked steps, calling on Goddess Ganga. Their prayers are perfectly juxtaposed with the long-drawn cry from the conch shells and the bells echoing from the temples.

At dusk, banks like that of Chandi Ghat will turn into funeral pyres as saffron-silk-wrapped corpses, brought in by devotees from all over India, will be cremated, their ashes fed to the holy Ganges so as to free their souls from the eternal cycle of birth and rebirth. And in this whirlwind of a town, between death and dirt, a few other professions live on.

I seek a *yatrawal* lounging by a lassi shop—the one who guides pilgrims and arranges hotel and travel bookings in this holy city for a few coins. His work is a cross between geography and geometry—charting the smoothest and shortest route between the chaotic ghats. He leads the way out of the street, through lanes that can barely allow a cat to squeeze through, trespassing the private backyards of homes. After a whole hour, the streets open on to the non-motorable Kusha Ghat—a riverbank with steps leading down to the water.

A footbridge runs over the piers, just above the waters where people bathe. A family tumbles out of a few hand-pulled rickshaws. The people are from Lucknow, one can tell from their smooth Urdu-laced accent. Leaving their bags at the banks, they step down into the cold river, immersing the children along with themselves. With one arm clutching their babies, the women of the family make their way into the water, dexterously slithering in and out of their saris and blouses. The yatrawal guides us only till the end of this ghat, eager to cater to the big family from Lucknow. 'I heard from a coolie at the train station that they wanted to stay overnight in Haridwar. Hotels are hard to get in the tourist season so I might as well chalk up a good commission for finding them decent rooms,' he tells me, sniggering, and saunters towards them, pointing us in the direction of our destination. A row of trees obscure the narrow passage leading up to it—their aerial roots turned into multiple trunks over hundreds of years of its existence, the trees that have seen it all.

'Mahendra Kumarji Panda *kahan milenge*?' I ask a sadhu with a long, grey chimerical beard, sipping chai at a counter in the passageway.

'Hmm,' he says eyeing my Dictaphone and diary with a look synonymous with other working men in Haridwar—a controlled smile that is swift and sharp, absorbing it all. He assumes a crouching position and says, 'I can see lot of negative field in your aura—sucking all your energy out.'

Perhaps he is referring to my dark circles. 'I can summon the ghosts of your ancestors to remedy this, if you want. It won't cost much.'

He insists, 'Try, it will help you understand your past life.' I look at him warily, taking in the faux leopard-skin skirt tied around his waist, his dreadlocks and his ash-smeared face. When he starts chanting indistinct words, I furiously shake my head.

'No?' He sighs and then says, 'Okay. Can you see that peepul tree? Mahendra sits in a room below it.'

Haridwar is a pilgrimage site for Hindus to cremate their kinfolk and meet the Pandas[2]—priests who double up as genealogists. They are in charge of the family register, of updating the family's genealogical tree with details of marriages, births and deaths, and so on.

The Pandas also arrange religious ceremonies for their clients and solemnize certain life-cycle rituals such as death ceremonies. The reason for their existence has to do with the Hindu belief that the family is everlasting and comprehensive and that each Hindu must look out for his ancestors and perform ceremonies for their journey after death to heaven.

In the spiderweb of little roads, Mahendra Kumar Panda, dressed in a white kurta, sits within a tube-light-lit box of a room on a mattress. He is a rotund, serious old man in his mid-sixties, with a vermillion tilak seen somewhere between the wrinkles on his forehead. Mathri bai from Bikaner has come to make offerings in memory of her dead husband. The grey eyes in her dull and time-worn face fill with tears. 'I can now die peacefully,' she says, sighing heavily as the Panda pockets a thick wad of cash.

For six years, Mathri bai had essentially walled herself in her hut after her husband passed away. This frail white-sari-draped widowed woman denied herself the joys of watching her grandchildren grow, of the everyday sun, all because her financial status did not let her perform the customary last rites for her husband in Haridwar. The travel was expensive and her family Panda had to be offered a donation worthy of her family's high-caste social background. So for those six years, she was absorbed in a religious reverie of pujas and bhajans within the four walls of her room while her thoughts circled around a sin so horrific that she was convinced she would go to hell for it.

Mathri bai finally took a loan from her younger sister to reach Haridwar, and once inside the alley, she was able to locate her family Panda amongst the thousand such men—so well networked are these men. The moment she entered the road, strangers barraged her with the mandatory questions asked of anyone who wants to search for a Panda in Haridwar.

'Which village did your ancestors belong to?'

'What is your husband's *gotra* [clan]?'

Once she answered the questions, the strangers pointed out Mahendra Kumar's office amidst the other Pandas' chambers.

On one wall of the room, alongside fat lizards, dust-ridden, garlanded black-and-white portraits of two stern-looking moustachioed men hang. 'My father, Sitaramji Panda, and his father, Ramnathji Panda,' Mahendera says, looking up at his ancestors; their watchful eyes seem to be shrewdly scrutinizing his, bestowing a latent chill to the otherwise balmy room. Mahendra grunts at them, as if admonishing them for prying, and then settles deeper into the mattress, firmly asserting his place in his ancestors' room.

'These genealogical registers have been with our family for many generations,' he reveals, his gravelly voice thick with indignation. 'You'll find us and our like in most pilgrimage places like Kashi, Varanasi, Gaya, but Haridwar continues to remain the most comprehensive and well-preserved repository,' he proudly adds, his large, soft-looking stomach moving in tandem with his speech.

The loss of roots of families, like the extinction of a species, is irrevocable. Sometimes, genealogical documentation was undertaken to maintain a sense of community within the religious threshold and at other times for the purposes of research; different record-keeping methods have been used across the world. But barring a few, most have been victims of one disaster or the other. More than half the citizens of London died in the Great Plague,[3] but most of their death records maintained by the parish were destroyed in the Great Fire of London the following year. Dr Lo Hsiang-lin, a renowned researcher in the Hakka language and culture, had built up an invaluable collection of Chinese-clan genealogies, but had to leave them behind when he fled to Hong Kong during the

Communist coup. These priceless documents were later thought to have been used by grocers as wrapping paper.[4]

Considering that more than 90 per cent of this world has slipped into an absolute torpor, with identities having been lost, and no particular written proof by which we might hope to find the names of everybody who has ever lived, this record-keeping method of the Pandas becomes a critical treasure trove of information—of recent human history, migratory patterns and even cultural evolution.

Over time, these dynastic records have also become a particularly important way of sorting out all the inheritance squabbles that arise for wealth and power in India. Mahendra Panda himself has issued affidavits with an oath commissioner's stamp to solve legal disputes of his *jajman*, or customers. 'I have been dragged to court a number of times,' he says, pausing, turning to produce a few stamped papers, his belly jiggling wildly in response to the movement. Dropping his voice to a hoarse whisper, he adds, 'People come from all parts of the world looking for their ancestral Panda—either to have them as witness in some property dispute, to attest to someone's actual last name, or to establish relationships between brothers, fathers and cousins. A few years ago,' he recalls, 'cousins from this particular family were fighting over property. Now, because the family was devout and were regulars here, I not only helped in issuing an affidavit but also went to court, all the way near Delhi, as a witness. That's the power Pandas have.' He shrugs, tossing the stamped papers aside with a contrived nonchalance, ineffectively trying to cloak the pride prospering on his bulbous nose. 'The court recognizes us as official geologists!'

'You mean genealogist?' I respond.

'Yes, yes . . . that thing,' he says, waving his hand dismissively. 'These books have been passed on to me and my brother from our *nana*ji. It's a responsibility we have. He didn't have any sons, only four daughters. So he distributed all the books amongst us,' he says.

'So this is a man's job?'

'Absolutely. Women can't enter this profession because they are not the legal heirs of these registers. These are only passed on to male legal heirs like sons and grandsons.' He scoffs, surprised that I would ask a question with such an obvious answer.

'*Suniye*, these books are an everyday livelihood for us, our cash cows. Over time, they can also be traded and sold. Such is their value that they can also be used as collateral against loans. So a man with no male lineage will pass it on to a male family member through his daughter, but never to the daughter herself.' His Brahmin head shakes in disapproval, a small tuft of hair tied into a tail wagging along with his head. And then, with a brittle smile, he crows, 'You know, as they say, a laughing Brahmin, a female Panda and a coughing thief are all destroyers of their race.'

He calls out to his young help, a matchstick-thin teen who left his village a few years ago to find clerical work, but in vain. The Panda finally came to his rescue and offered him food and a small pay for odd jobs. He stands, now, outside the door with his hips slanted against the wall and, as part of his instructions, casually shoots the breeze with prospective customers about his employer's glorious, connate connection with Goddess Ganga and the powerful mantras he gives his customers. All this with a smile plastered on his lips that completely belies his grudging trudge into the office soon after.

'*Aaram se* . . . [Be careful],' Mahendra Kumar chides him as the fellow tries different keys from a bundle, the handle of the inbuilt iron safe squawking as it turns, the rust layered over the years grinding at its hinges. 'I give you money to help, not to break my precious furniture,' the Panda says, wriggling his eyebrows, as the boy pulls open the safe from which emanates a smell of times gone by—of paper decaying in the dampness of centuries-old closets. 'Never trust a Bhangi,' he whispers to me sideways, referring to the young boy's caste.

In the caste world of Haridwar, the Panda's moneyless help belonged to the lowest South Indian caste, Bhangi, whereas the Pandas were much higher in the societal structure. Mahendra Panda, like most of his ilk, inhabited the role of his Brahmin caste with incontestable gravity.

Pulling out two elongated registers, called *vahi*s, from a pile of about a hundred-odd files—all about twelve-inches thick and encased in jute covers—from the depths of the safe, the boy places them before the Panda, sending a cloud of dust flying. The Panda puts on his round gold-rimmed spectacles, making him look earnest, vulnerable even, as he carefully sifts through the loosened pages of the books.

There are entries of an old business family from Rajasthan whose kin have spread far and wide—to tiny villages in Bihar, to the hills beyond Coimbatore and to the bustling metropolises of Hyderabad and Bangalore. Then there is a Punjabi family from Amritsar with eight sons and their respective family trees. And another one from Gujarat whose pet dog has been listed too. The entries are in Urdu, Sanskrit, Hindi and various other regional scrawls by literate pilgrims and, in other cases, by the Panda himself. 'Families have changed their religion over the years. A few Muslims switched to Hinduism. Some who were brought up in Lahore were Hindus but could write only in the local dialect, Urdu,' he explains, peering above his spectacles at the multilingual vahis.

'I still get jajman from the Kathat community[5] in Rajasthan; it follows both Hindu and Muslim traditions. They bury their dead in the ground close to their homes, but come here for their last rites and to update the records.' These registers also became important genealogical sources for many splintered Hindu families, aiding them in tracing their family tree and family history, especially after the Partition in 1947 and, later, amongst the Indian diaspora which migrated to America, Australia and even Trinidad and Tobago and Fiji.

'Let's look for your history now,' he says, pulling open one of the two vahis. With time-honoured dexterity, he leafs through the scroll with my family's genealogy, its pages scrawled with names and dates. 'So your ancestral village is Ladnun in Rajasthan, you said?'

I nod.

'Hmmm . . . And the caste?' he asks.

Pulling open a sheaf of paper with notes from my father, I inform him that my caste is Oswal.

'Okay, and the gotra is Dugar,' he reads aloud as he scans the documents.

Pandas arrange these documents first by the village from which the ancestors hail, followed by the gotra from that village—the Oswals would be in one section, the Agarwals in another and then the Maheshwaris. This enables a Panda to name a pilgrim's family and ancestors with no information other than the pilgrim's first name, last name, gotra and ancestral village.

The basis of this classification also helps in defining the community and its descendants and to derive the areas of incest. This is especially useful in arranged marriages in India where one has to marry within the same caste—for example, an Oswal cannot marry within the same gotra, in this instance, with a Dugar.

'Look at the ink that we used for writing back then. It's a pure Brahmin product,' he says, looking up from the book, referring to the rich, dark sooty ink that seems to conjure its own story—of large cauldrons over hot coals and bare-bodied Brahmin men stirring through it, their bodies luminous not with stinky sweat but with age-old wisdom. 'Once made,' the Panda continues, 'the ink was offered to Ganga Maiyya.' A few drops in the river during a puja. 'The ink had rich ingredients like almond peels and sap from banana trees for longevity.' He smiles proudly.

'You do not make this ink any more?' I ask.

'Well, who has the time? And yes, the ingredients can be a bit unaffordable these days, so we make do with the locally available stuff in the markets. Anyway, don't you want to look at your family records?' He snaps, muttering something about a family from Punjab that was due to visit him any time now. He finally opens the page to my family tree. A list of members of the family running back five generations unfolds, with the dates of their death, the relative who came to perform the last rites and their respective signatures. Disappointingly, only a few of my female ancestors are listed in the records. But it's hard to supress the joy of seeing a tangible link with my own history, one that I can perhaps pass down to my children some day.

Nobody will be conducting me to the Hindu heavens just because my ancestral history lies with this man whose community is sometimes branded as charlatans using religion to swindle the naive. After all, from a pragmatic viewpoint, they seem to be obtaining lot of money and respect for merely writing a line or two for each family, perhaps twice in a decade—or thrice if misfortune strikes. But at the same time, Mahendra Panda is the man who maintains my family's death records, ensuring for me a little sense of my roots and a robust sense of history.

My great-grandfather is only a name and a few photographs to me, but I remember my grandfather and loved his stories of the days of yore, including a few about his father—the burly, authoritarian owner of jute fields who switched off all the lights in the house before he went to sleep, regardless of when the rest of his family went to bed. He spoke of his two cousins who poked a pair of scissors through their own eyes in separate incidents, and his brother with whom he often played *kushti*.

I first came to know about these records from this same kushti-loving brother of my grandfather. He had come to Haridwar to immerse my grandfather's ashes when he died, like his ancestors had done. His signature, a thumbprint, is stamped over my grandfather's date of death in Mahendra Kumar's vahi. 'It's incredible,' my grandfather's brother had said when we last met. 'Those weren't the times of Facebook and instant messaging. I had forgotten the names of a few of my ancestors and there they were in the records. We got in touch with our extended cousins soon after and met at a wedding.'

Curious to know how relationships between Pandas and families were established, I ask Mahendra Panda how our ancestors chose a particular Panda.

'You don't choose a Panda; a Panda chooses you,' he snorts. 'It is a hereditary relationship ultimately defined by the jajman's paternal ancestral home. So those who live in Jodhpur and its surrounding areas are handled by a particular Panda because this Panda has developed relationships with them as they came for their pilgrimages. Somewhere along the way, the records of Jodhpuri citizens would get divided along the way and be distributed among, say, three Pandas who were his sons, each having a selection of gotras. So if you know the region and the gotra you come from, we know which Panda to direct to you to,' he explains.

'During my grandfather's times, most people came by foot, travelling for months on end through forests and hinterland,' Mahendra Kumar recalls, pulling out a picture of his office from the days of the horse and buggy—a monochrome picture of a small cubicle made of *khus* sheets, with his grandfather sitting on a chair outside it. 'Many of these pilgrims died because surrounding Haridwar were jungles infested with dacoits, tigers, elephants and diseases.'

'So I have five generations listed here. What is the earliest record you have of others?' I ask.

'Some records go back to 1799, but before that they used to write in this now-lost form of record-keeping known as the *bhojpatra*,[6] on the barks of the Himalayan birch tree. We used to inscribe the details on the bark and place them in layers of cloth. This was before the Mughal emperor Akbar introduced paper in the sixteenth century. Nobody seems to have these bhojpatras any more. They were delicate and sensitive to weather changes. We didn't have iron safes back then.'

Besides the vahis written by the Pandas, India has other forms of genealogical records too—such as those maintained by the Manganiyars,[7] the singing community from Rajasthan that make *shubhraj*, which is a sort of panegyric. Then there are *panji*s, the extensive genealogical records maintained among Maithil Brahmins in Bihar. But, by far, the most extensive and widespread records are those maintained by the Pandas, especially the ones in Haridwar.

The oldest records with the Pandas come from the neighbouring states of Uttar Pradesh, Rajasthan and Punjab, which each have strong links with Haridwar, possibly because of their trade route. Meanwhile, records from the eastern region of India, like Bihar, appear only in the late-eighteenth century, thanks to the growth of the railways in 1886. Most of the earlier records are of the status-conscious Brahmins, which the Pandas themselves ensured they recorded, so as to secure potential future patronage to these high-caste moneyed landlords. Soon, families from castes lower than that of the Brahmins started undertaking expensive pilgrimages to Haridwar, serving their status aspirations, elaborate death rituals being one of the prime ways of showing hierarchy in society.

A Punjabi family soon gathers outside Mahendra Kumar's door. They have made an overnight journey by train from Sonam, Punjab. One of their kin has passed away, the help explained to me later, and his last wish was for his body to float down the Ganga. 'Jai Ganga Maiyyaji,'[8] the Panda greets them, smiling broadly—a mysterious beaming that seems to have a larger meaning, putting one in the awkward position of trying to figure out what that meaning could be.

Giving instructions to his help to serve tea, the Panda turns to pack things up so that he can take the family to the ghats for the last rites. 'They are a religious family, this one. They come to me after every death in the family. For them I am the *kul purohit*, and I am summoned to their village for every religious ritual. I get such people from everywhere—Jodhpur zilla, Ajmer zilla, Beawar . . .'

'Who takes care of your work when you are gone?' I ask as we walk out to the bank. Beads of sweat form on his brow in spite of the cool breeze; the drops loosen and trickle down, like the old man's future. 'My brother's son Prashant will take care of my *gaddi* after I'm gone. He sits here from nine in the morning to seven in the evening and then goes back to our place in Jwalapur. Most of the married Pandas live there to maintain the sanctity of Ma Ganga's Haridwar—since relationships in the bed are prohibited here,' he whispers, his breath shortening. 'It's a two-hundred-year-old gaddi. Someone has to maintain this legacy,' he adds, looking out at the river shining under the sun, despite the filth beneath. 'My two sons work in Bangalore in banks.'

'Won't they take up your job?'

'No, no. They can't all sit in the same room, right?'

The times are changing, and the family trees in these ancient books may soon be quaint relics. The scientific world view is increasingly eating into the Pandas' work, raising greater doubts about the value of ritual and religious actions. Some Pandas feel bound to their clients by way of inherited religious pledges, and for financial reasons. But few things have changed in their record-keeping methodology over time; being a traditionalist community, they are averse to change and resort to conventional methods of record-keeping. Many have dropped out of the profession, finding lucrative options in the growing tourism industry in Haridwar as hotel managers and owners. But except a few, most Pandas rebuff the idea of making all their records public.

The information in the vahis could be used against their clients, one hears, or could undermine some of the Pandas' own claims that the records are their inheritance if they could possibly be purchased from other Panda families. Even the Genealogical Society of Utah[10] has microfilmed about 500 vahis since 1977, when they first undertook this project in India as part of their genealogical research project spanning the globe. Pandas, who are technologically averse, are wary of this research, and most refuse to share their records, fearing that multiple copies will be made, possibly resulting in them losing their everyday livelihood—in spite of the fact that the contracts are drawn between the society and the Panda and state that they will not 'sell, assign, give, or part [with them] in any way . . . except with the prior written permission of the Compiler [the Panda].'

When I ask him about the films at Utah, Mahendra Kumar clicks his tongue in disapproval. 'I refused to give it to them. Everything in Haridwar these days is done keeping foreigners in mind,' he rants. 'A lot of our Pandas gave away their details, but I don't think they are secure. They want to make a . . . what do you call it . . . yes, a website of it. There is a legacy associated with this work; it is what the gods have asked us to do. You can't commercialize everything. But it's not completely their fault. More generally, it is the moral corruption that the market has unleashed on everything. They want to wear Western clothes, listen to Angrezi songs and eat Italian . . .'

In that instant it is hard to tell if these are purely the maudlin yearnings of an ageing man, or whether Haridwar really has undergone as much globalization as he claims. Then, suddenly, the Panda catches me by surprise and says, '*Kaafi fayde bhi hain in websites ke; wahaan koi aapse caste nahi mangega* [There are benefits to the website as well; no one asks you your caste there].' He cackles to hide his mounting panic.

We arrive at the ghat where families hold each other's hands at the steps while the water rushes past them—green and viscous, sometimes like an oil slick. Piles of flowers, varying containers of ghee, red cloths used for rituals and other refuse bobs in the water by the pier.

'Would you want buy your own computer to keep a more permanent electronic copy of the records?' I ask him, wary of facing his wrath.

But he smiles instead. 'Would you come to me if I wrote these records on fancy computers instead of in these legendary old books? I don't know, really, how many more generations will continue this work. But I will live by this holy Ganga till I die. It is a duty bestowed on us by the Gods . . . How can I run away from it?' he says, darkly, staring at his own reflection in the rushing waters, each wave washing it away, leaving behind a mere bleak grey silhouette.

People have trod this way for centuries now, along the banks of the Ganga. At the main ghat, barbers shave the heads of the men from the Punjabi family, to signify mourning, while the Panda gives them his blessings. He then summons a Mahapatra sitting under an umbrella by the ghat, who quickly puts out his chillum. 'Now, this is the only way for poor men to relax. We don't earn thousands from customers, do we?' The red-eyed man with a hunchback mocks the Panda, who, in turn, stands a few feet away from him, turning a deaf ear.

The Pandas themselves do not perform any rites for the first twelve days after a death. Instead, they pass on the work to the Mahapatras who help the men of the family light cotton wicks soaked in ghee, snuggled in a basket made of leaves and marigolds, flickering as they go downstream—amidst a hundred other such vessels sent out by many other sons, brothers, nephews and uncles, honouring their dead in this dark, muddy water, reeking of death and decay. The Panda closes his eyes, swaying back and forth, lips moving furiously as he chants the mantras.

And then, just like Lord Bhagiratha laboured to pull down the Ganges from paradise so that the river's holy touch would release his ancestors from the cycle of birth and death in the Ramayana, the men pour out the ashes from a brass pot, feeding it to the holy river. Once, a humming, gurgling eager river with crystal-clear water that purified one's body and soul, it is now just an endless convoy of din and dirt, dung and death, where men, women, Pandas and the dead, all immerse themselves in its cold, mythical embrace.

4

THE KABOOTARBAAZ
OF OLD DELHI

Pigeons were the bane of our existence in the years growing up. A pigeon would often sit on our room's window ledge, its grubby feathers and excrement propelling in every direction. It would coo its imprudent brains out with an eerie, unnerving, bone-chilling sound that announced its arrival every morning at 5.45 a.m., like clockwork. This would be followed by my sister and I aiming all the pillows we had at the window on the bed to send the bird flying off the ledge, only to hear it return and coo again within the next five minutes—wagging its tail, blinking its deceptively innocent eyes, bobbing its neck forward, craning its neck, scavenging for leftover food in bins and gutters and adapting almost too well to our urban environment.

Life is brief, especially with eagles and electrical poles around, so the pigeon stuffed itself with vegetable peels from the rubbish bin and pickles left out in to dry in the sun. It established itself in the neighbourhood trees, its droppings coating the branches like thick sleet. One fine day, it laid eggs in the corner between the air cooler and the wall in spite of the spikes installed on the sill—and then there was a whole family of them. We knew the worst was upon us. It was war!

Our domestic help poked into the pigeons' empty nest with long brooms and knocked it off. Nets were installed between the windows and we even kept a bottle of water with liquid detergent handy to spray them off the ledges. About a month later, the 'plumed rats' were finally gone, but they didn't merely disappear from the windowsill. They vanished from the other homes in the colony and every tree, electrical wire and veranda in between. The neighbourhood gathered at the community hall for a pigeon-themed party, complete with paper beaks and a cake with a model pigeon perched on it, but we still ended up waking up every day at 5.45 a.m. for weeks after that. A few months on, we saw an impressive white pigeon indulging in histrionics at a local mela and suddenly felt guilty for the loss of this familiar creature.

Many years later, here I am in a locality behind Jama Masjid in Old Delhi—a sprawling neighbourhood of large rooftops. In the spaces between a low sky dotted with the blackened facades of homes and a crazy mishmash of thick and thin cable wires hanging like an upturned bowl of noodles between buildings, I can see large flocks of pigeons. In the mellow rays of the November sun they are wheeling around, turning and swooping in unison—like obedient wooden puppets manipulated on a string for this wonderfully coordinated performance. On the roofs of the buildings, some unwalled, men are whistling, tooting and shrieking at the birds, mouthing directions. They are the puppeteers, the walled city's renowned *kabootarbaaz*, racing their pet pigeons in the vast, open skies.

'I can take you up to one of those rooftops. They keep a lot of pigeons at homes,' offers one of the two young boys, still in their school uniforms, puttering about on the streets to avoid the evening shift at their father's brass shop. The boy instantly recognizes the address I give him of a pigeon flier. 'He is the best kabootarbaaz of Old Dilli,' he screams over the noise, walking us through the dense battlefield-like streets of Chawri Bazaar—labourers rushing by with their laden backs, rickshaws plying schoolchildren and scooters floundering through streets lined with copper, brass and paper shops with one-room apartments squeezed in between.

Kabootarbaazi, or pigeon fancying, finds its first mention in history in the fifth Aegyptian dynasty, in about 3000 BC,[1] when people raised them in conical mud coops. Excavations made in Shivta, an ancient abandoned city in Negev Desert in Israel, revealed dovecotes both above and below the ground for pigeon-breeding activities, dating back to the Middle Ages.

In India, pigeon keeping and racing enjoyed great patronage when pigeons were sent as gifts by the kings of I´rán and Túrán; merchants also brought in excellent pigeons in large numbers. According to tradition, the *kulkulain*, or competitions, began when the birds were taken to a faraway spot and released to the sound of a shotgun being fired, announcing the beginning of the race.

Pigeons, with their remarkable ability to navigate perfectly over journeys of several hundred miles, raced their way back home in flocks, guiding each other, sticking together like family. After calculating the distance to the homes of the pigeon owners, the winners were declared upon the arrival of the flocks. Several organizers were stationed at specific points to take stock of how far each pigeon had flown and the corresponding time frame. The first pigeon that completed the route and returned to its proud owner was declared the winner. Nobody is certain precisely how the birds pulled this feat off and still continue to do so. The maudlin reasoning is that if pigeons like where they live, they employ all their visceral predispositions—along with sight, smell, sound, magnetic fields and taste. But recent research reveals that pigeons use 'odour maps',[2] associating the routes with smell, and travel with them.

Emperor Jahangir spent days in the company of kabootarbaaz, learning the age-old tricks of pigeon-flying like his father, Akbar,[3] who was also very fond of the sport and had many thousands of pigeons in his court as well as his country retreats like Nagarchain near Agra[4]. He may have perhaps inherited his love of pigeons from his grandfather Babur and his father, Umar Sheikh Mirza, who was a pigeon fancier too.

Akbar referred to the pastime as *ishkbazi*,[5] and his favourite pigeon was called Mohanah, which became the chief of the imperial pigeons; from it descended several excellent pigeons such as Ashkí (the weeper), Parízád (the fairy), Almás (the diamond) and Sháh'údí (Aloe Royal), and their progeny were again the choicest pigeons in the whole world. Pigeons, back then, were trained to execute fairly complicated manoeuvres including the wheel (charkha), 'a lusty movement ending with the pigeon throwing itself over in a full circle' and turning somersaults (*bazi*). In Akbar's court, a select pigeon could perform fifteen charkhas and seventy bazis in one session. The Jesuit priest Father Monserrate,[6] in his book *The Commentary of Father Monserrate on His Journey to the Court of Akbar*, writes: 'The pigeons are cared for by eunuchs and servant-maids. Their evolutions are controlled at will, when they are flying, by means of certain signals, just as those of well-trained soldiery are controlled by a competent general by means of bugles and drums. It will seem little short of the miraculous when I affirm that, when sent out, they dance, turn somersaults all together in the air, fly in orderly rhythm, and return to their starting point, all at the sound of a whistle.'

The Mughal emperor Bahadur Shah Zafar's state processions in the seventeenth century through the streets of Shahjahanabad, now known as Old Delhi, always included an elephant that lugged the imperial pigeon cage with some top-notch breeds, the prices of which were also decided by the Mughal court, making them a much-coveted possession—almost every noble owned a *kabootarkhana* in their home back then.

Centuries later, a few bird lovers still pursue this ancient interest on the same streets. But the streets that were once known to house resplendent dancing girls[7] have gradually been taken over by markets with thousands of shops that spring up everywhere in Delhi, like fungus after the rains. As we walk down the streets, the blue skies over Chawri Bazaar are blocked by ceilings. We turn down an alley and start ascending the staircase of a gloomy concrete building. The walls of the building seem to be necrotic, as if affected by a blackening disease. Open urinals and spittoons have been added to the staircase landings years after the construction of the building, as an afterthought. The dark, high staircase finally opens on to the fourth floor to Anil Sood's rooftop which stands in stark contrast to the rest of the building—it's surprisingly clean, spacious, and with impossibly white parapets. The city noises fade to a distant hum here—the air growing thinner, cooler. The Jama Masjid, the Pashupatinath temple and the Gurdwara Sis Ganj Sahib jut out amidst the rooftops and half-abandoned homes of Old Delhi. God, they say, is closer when you're on one of these rooftops.

Sood is a kabootarbaaz who keeps thousands of pigeons as pets on this rooftop. He is one of the few ustads, an honorific title that is bestowed by the commune in Old Delhi for racing feats, prowess and, in his case, for the over twenty-five years of experience he has. But he is hardly one of your regular bird lovers—the sort who wears a safari jacket, a fragile being with kind eyes, tottering around hill stations, with binoculars draped around the neck and carting a thick copy of *The Ultimate Bird Lover: Stories and Advice on Our Feathered Friends at Home and in the Wild*. Sood, on the other hand, is barely literate, having dropped in and out of school. On most Fridays he would slip out of his father's clutches to visit the pigeon market behind Jama Masjid. He is tall, gym-built, with muscles bulging everywhere.

In the afternoon sun, here on the rooftop, Sood's naked eyes dampen from staring into the sky for too long, brown irises suspended in webs of red wires. '*Aao, aao,*' he calls out, a hand imitating the scattering of seeds. Within seconds, birds that were little more than flecks in the sky appear, the soft flapping of their wings soon becoming a thunderous roar. And when the flock finally flaps down on to the rooftop, about twenty of them together, Anil screams, 'Yes, winner!' Anil's birds have just won the race, taking the shortest time to arrive from Ghaziabad— less than fifteen minutes—using the odour maps of their neighbourhood to orient themselves. Three other flocks competing from Old Delhi take a lot more time, some late almost by an hour.

Over the years, Sood's pigeons, especially this lot swooping down on his rooftop, of the Punjabi Patiala breed, have won various wagers. The Golas from Agra or the Madrasis from Gwalior are no match for them.

Days before the race, Sood's apprentices and compeers gather on his rooftop, practising in the evenings, followed by games of rummy, a few beers and dirty jokes. There is no gathering of owners today because everyone wants to see their flocks come back to their coops. But as soon as the birds arrive, a group of Sood's fans, mostly comprising his apprentices, cruise up to the rooftop, eager for phone videos of the winning *tukda* of birds. Mithai boxes are opened and laddus are passed around. Marigold garlands are hung around Sood's neck until it droops, and men cosy up to him to learn a few tricks of the trade.

'I purchased this *nasal* for a fortune from an Amritsari *kabootar* wallah. *Koi mazak ki baat nahi hai* [It is no joke],' he announces to his audience as the birds toddle away obligingly into the dovecote at the rear of the roof.

'This comes from a lot of experience, bhai. How will I teach you in a day?'

'*Ab mere kabootron ko nazar lag jayegi. Bas bhi karo. Chasme Badoor* [My pigeons might become victims of your evil eye. Stop it now. Far be the evil eye.]' He shoos them all away with an air of self-gratification.

Soon the crowd fades away, leaving Sood and his helpers to tend to the birds. Getting rid of the garlands, Sood picks up a brown pigeon; it has injured its wing, and a red gash runs down to its muscle. 'The birds sometimes kill themselves,' he remarks, his voice hoarse from all the shouting. 'When large flocks descend on rooftops, the younger birds that land first are squashed under the mass of the latecomers,' he says, gently stroking the injured pigeon's neck. He has, in the past, lost a bird to hawks and another to bad weather, and a few more to a flu that spread through the birds in the neighbourhood; but this time, just one came back scathed.

'They are far safer in the cages than outside,' he says, making kissy faces at the bird. 'Most of our birds live up to fifteen years in here, but strays survive for no more than five years out there.' Holding the bird firmly in his hands, he walks towards the edge of the roof and flings the pigeon into the sky. The pigeon takes an instant to balance itself, flaps its wings in a concerted effort and then bursts upwards for a few moments, becomes unsteady and flutters right back on to his arm.

'It may have crashed into a slit cable wire,' he murmurs, summoning his help to pull up a bench for us. 'I keep them like my family,' he says with fondness, pointing towards a large cage packed with a variety of pigeons and covered by a mesh. The dark skin on his hand is covered halfway up by a bright-orange linen shirt, matching the orange chappals adorning his feet; his gold rings add to his swagger, while his shirt collar is pulled up in an oddly irrepressible way.

'One evening, I came back from work and found that my favourite pigeon had died. It was of this breed, Hyderabadi Junglay—one of my prized possessions. I was absolutely shattered and was going to sew its feathers on to my cap. I had left it on the parapet and went looking for a cloth to bury it in; I returned to see a cat sniffing it for a meal,' he says, tapping the bird's beak. 'I flung the cat off the parapet and it fell on the roof below us, meowing its stupid brains out. It broke a paw, I think.' Anil looks up, baring his paan-stained canines in a grin, exuding a somewhat louche cool.

He inherited his love for these birds from his family who have been flying pigeons for five generations now. 'My ancestors could recognize the breed of a pigeon just by inspecting its droppings,' he says proudly.

He likes to tell the story of his grandfather, a multiple-award-winning flier of his day. 'After Independence, he took up his belongings, took a rickshaw from his home in Mehrauli and came here to Old Delhi. All he carried were twelve pigeons in a cage which he hid beneath his seat.' But the pigeons refused to call his Old Delhi flat home. 'Pigeons are like posters of Madhuri Dixit that you stick on the walls with Fevicol and refuse to peel off when you decide to shift, loyalties,' he says, laughing. 'Their first instinct the moment they are let out is to fly back home. They flew back to Mehrauli where my grandfather used to live with his brother. The brother notified him a few days later through a telegram that said: "They are hungry all the time. I can't give them so much time. Come and get them."'

Anil learnt the craft from his father, Ramkishan Sood. His father taught him how to capture another man's flock and direct it home like a herd of lambs. He taught him to fly these birds like an airplane, with techniques to direct the pigeons to any place he liked. 'I remember this one day when his friends had come over.'

Anil's father was a *khalifa*, a master of the field—but lower in ranking than an ustad—and had multiple disciples training under him. 'They were talking about a kit of *safed* [white] kabootar that my father had purchased just then. These white birds had an excellent memory and great homing instincts. *Maine socha ise aazmayenge* [I thought, let's test this theory]. And I set the birds free to see if they would come back to their loft. But, of course, they were not trained. They didn't consider our home as their home yet and flew away, perching on that red dome of the Jama Masjid,' he says, pointing in the direction of the smog-covered monument. 'My father beat me up, black and blue, worse than the first thrashing he'd given when he had caught me smoking. If some other kabootarbaaz caught the safed kabootar, he'd mate them with his local birds and make their breed plebeian. Three days later, the safed kabootar came back and my father gave me another slap to ensure that I never forgot my lesson.' He laughs. 'That was the first and last time I made that mistake.'

Calm has descended over this orange hour of the afternoon, interrupted only by a soft, pained flutter of wings from the injured bird. The help brings Sood a brass plate of pellets—a home-made remedy of powdered turmeric and ghee. Pellet by pellet, he feeds it to the injured pigeon. 'You experience what it is like to have a child dependent on you,' Sood says after a long pause. 'They need love and attention, these things, and thrive under it. If it wasn't for them, I'd probably be involved in petty gang wars on the streets like most other young men here,' he says softly without looking up.

Anil grew up in Chawri Bazaar's black-and-white underbelly—a world of crooks and paltry politicians, of brothels and small-time criminals.

'I'd sneak up to the rooftop and train my father's birds—away from the real-estate business I was trying to establish,' Sood says.

At first, the pigeons lived in a small, old wooden cage without a mesh. After Sood's collection grew and it became difficult to tread through it without crunching on pigeon feed, a larger dovecote was constructed with wire mesh, separate cages and wooden lofts.

Inside, the coop is tiny but clean, echoing with the odd, almost silent sound of the birds, like a breeze passing through a leafy tree. Tiny bangles adorn the feet of the birds—shiny coloured beads strung together, tinkling as they waddle around—a marker of the ownership of the bird. 'This is the Hyderabadi Junglay,' Sood says, picking them up and rotating them in all possible ways so that we can see their wings, feet and eyes, remarking on each one's potential with the thoroughness of a diamond trader at the jewellery shops in the streets below. 'This one's texture is excellent,' he says, pointing to a pigeon with a bright chestnut-coloured breast and granite back, a dusting of incandescence around its neck that sometimes appears fuchsia and, in the sunlight, orange and jade.

'This white one, a Basra, is getting too fat. I have to reduce his ghee intake. The one with the fan on its rear is called Fantail and that is the Lahori.' Sood individually names his veritable empire of a thousand birds, comprising about thirty breeds in all. There are Indian, Russian, Afghan and Burmese pigeons, and some breeds from countries the names of which he can't even pronounce. 'These are Helmets. They can fly for thirteen to fourteen hours without a pause,' he adds as he takes out a lovely brown specimen from the birdcage with sorrel-coloured eyes. My room is painted to match its eyes. *Sundar hai na* [Isn't it beautiful]?' he asks, misty-eyed.

On Friday evenings, Sood walks down a few metres to the foot of the Jama Masjid as the sounds of the Maghrib prayers float from one masjid in the area to another, as if passing on news about him and his expensive buys at the pigeon market every week. Sellers come from nearby towns and villages, their cages stuffed with birds of all shapes and colours. Kablis sells for Rs 300 while Basras and Roshan Chirags are priced between Rs 10,000–20,000.

Most of the crowd in the field consists of onlookers watching the kabootarbaz examine the birds, their flight and strength, scrutinizing their authenticity under a microscope and then haggling over the price. Some old-timers, meanwhile, find cosy spots on rocks jutting out of the hill and tell tales of pigeons from the times of kings and queens. Others indulge in marginal forms of employment—selling tea to weary traders, hawking strings with which to tie the legs of the bird. The market is also considered the perfect place for greenhorns to learn about pigeons, and for pesky teenagers who aren't entertained by the sellers to find solace in odd bits of revenge, sneaking up behind them to click open their cages, making the precious birds pour out like water, swirling towards sky, mostly towards the sellers' homes. Looking at them cranking open their much-suppressed wings, it is hard to believe they will find their way back home, or would even want to.

Sood, meanwhile, lets his pigeons loose for an hour everyday on his rooftop—to fly around, train and, sometimes, to just idle away in the warm winter sun. Three domestic help are hired on a monthly basis to scrape away bird droppings, hose down the cages, carry food up from Sood's kitchen below and refill the water canisters where the birds are let out to take a bath. A few bottles of essential oil are stocked in a box. Tubs of the pigeons' bathing water are laced with fragrant oils called *ittar* so that it is easy to identify the owner of the pigeons. 'It is a sign of status for us. We can smell the difference between genuine high-quality ittar from fifty feet away,' Sood remarks. 'This ittar, chameli *ke phool wallah* essence, made of crushed roses and jasmine flowers, is a fragrance that I had specially customized.'

Sood spends so much time on the roof that he has built himself a room here, outfitted with a fan, a television and a bed for naps. 'My birds need love and care all the time. They fall sick like little children, catch a cold, have flu and stomach upsets. There is this book I was passed on to by my grandfather—it has my great-grandfather's recipes of home-made medicines for pigeons,' he says, pulling out a diary covered in an oil cloth. Recipes in blue ink written in Hindi pop out of the yellowed pages. The book is smeared with crusty pigeon poop here and there.

For cold: Red chillies fried in clarified butter, ground fine and made into pellets with water. To be given for two days.

For instable legs in infancy: Mix the droppings of the pigeon with warm mustard oil and wrap its feet in it. Also, leave some earth in its loft for fulfilling its calcium needs.

For longer flying hours: Large cardamom, black pepper, sugar, fennel seeds, carom seeds, clove, bay leaf, betel leaf. Heat everything in water and bottle it. Feed the day the pigeon has to take a long flight.

A kit of pigeons who were a part of the race roll back across the sky, hurtling towards the clouds and then dive-bomb in perfect unison, splitting apart into two and integrating once again—like men and women swirling across the floor together in a ballroom dance. 'Look at that one,' Sood points to a dark pigeon straying away from the flock like a lonely cloud. 'This one will leave the flock because it is confused, going around in circles. Their kabootarbaaz should ideally keep him separate.' He clicks his tongue. Over the years, Sood has learnt that he should get rid of birds that frequently pull away from the flock because such rebels will lure birds into other flocks too. On a rooftop a few blocks away, their young kaboortabaaz Ahmad is frantically whistling and screeching, trying to lure the bird back into the flock. He holds his head in his hands dejectedly as the isolated pigeon separates himself from the group and joins Khalifa Jaggu dada's pigeons flying in from another direction.

Banging his fist against his hand, Sood laughs at him. 'The first three spots in the race are gone. Only the last spot is left. You are not winning this one. You have a long way to go,' he shouts at the amateur flier. When a pigeon from one group joins another, the original owner loses the right over that pigeon, only claiming it if he is ready to pay a compensation amount.

'My secret is that I keep all my pigeons separate—males in one coop, females in another.' This organization is termed 'widowhood', in which coupling pairs are kept in different cages to increase their yearning for each other—and, accordingly, to aid their hurriedness to get back home. 'Training,' he says, readjusting his collar again, 'is the toughest bit. You should always keep newborn pigeons, or squabs, in the coop for four weeks and only let them out when they are hungry so they will be trained to return.'

He explains further, 'It is important to know what to feed pigeons at a given time of the year. As the trees start shedding leaves in February and March, the birds start shedding feathers too. They are mostly in their cages then, mating and getting some family time. It is important to give them a diet of cooling liquids made of things such as khus-khus, the juice of almonds blended with water and bajra soaked in water.

'In the winters, we work on building their strength. This is the flying season, when we give them rotis. Flour is mixed with ghee to make dough and then fat rotis are rolled out,' he says. These are then baked on fire, skinned to remove the hard parts, and then crumbled to be fed to the pigeons. On the days the birds are expected to be airborne, the birds are given a rich diet of dry fruits like *kaju*, *badam* and spices like *elaichi* with clarified butter. 'Their mouths are designed to eat more than double. They eat almost two hundred grams a day,' he says, showing a steel measuring-cup designed for this purpose. 'They are brats, these kids.' Sood laughs. 'They will throw up all the food they ate earlier if they like something better.'

Sood spends between Rs 50,000–1,00,000 a month on taking care of these pigeons. *'Yeh nawabon ka shaukh hai ji. Aise thodi koi bhi pappu jhappu inhe palega* [This is a royal hobby. Not everyone can be a pigeon fancier]. I always knew my returns would be less. The only time I actually earn money is from competitions and, sometimes, when I sell squabs of a precious breed. For my grandfather, this was his part-time profession. He earned money from breeding, betting, selling these racing pigeons. But it can be as expensive as you want it to be. You can have fewer, local birds and spend less on their food and more on their training.'

Several pigeon societies evolved as pigeon racing turned from a hobby to a part-time profession, helping solve disputes and other matters. 'At these societies, we go to one another for good birds. We exchange notes on birds and also purchase them from pigeon fanciers in other cities like Chennai and Kolkata,' he says. Throughout the world, in Iran, Belgium, the United States, Pakistan and India, as many as one million people keep homing pigeons. Sood compares the atmosphere at these meetings to an Irani chai cafe, where 'men come to get away from their women and the pressures of the week'. The camaraderie often involves uncouth but good-natured mocking about how many birds a flier caught from another's flock. The chatter also allows for racial taunts, though some comments bite too hard. *'Arrey, tu who kale Madrasi log se haar gaya? Langot bandh le, langot* [You lost against those dark Madrasis? Time to wear a diaper, my boy]. Pigeon racing also has an unobserved felonious side to it. While the theft of cherished birds is common, gangs have been known to set fire to coops following rivalries and arguments about decisions at competitions.

As the Government of India does not permit[8] the import of these birds, some individuals and organizations that breed and train pigeons import eggs of particular bloodlines and hatch them—bypassing the law and stocking the European pigeons in various lofts. And like dogfighting, pigeon racing is often accursed with the problem of gambling. Animal rights organization People for the Ethical Treatment of Animals (PETA) penetrated racing organizations all over the world where thousands of dollars is bet on a single race, and discovered that pigeon racing generates huge amounts in illegal gambling and involves felony violations of racketeering and tax-evasion laws.

The high stakes can also lead some flyers to cheat. A young doctor who treats the birds close to Old Delhi, and who refused to be named, reveals that some birds failed tests for banned performance-enhancing drugs, even opium. 'Non-performing birds can be very expensive to maintain sometimes. Their treatment, food and nutrition are obligations. Often, their necks are wrung and their remains buried ignominiously.'

'It's flawed. This whole system is flawed,' screams Anil when we speak about it. 'These animal organizations that claim we torture these birds are on a witch hunt. Why would they keep returning to us if we tortured them? Anyway, the presence of drugs in the system of these birds doesn't give you an advantage. The bird has to be of a good breed and trained well. They are intelligent birds. Now look at that flock coming towards us,' he says, spotting another in the air. The other flocks of the neighbouring home are returning, one by one, some so large that they blot out the sun.

'If you look at them carefully, they somersault,' says Sood excitedly. 'These birds perform some of their best histrionics in the air, all for the fun of it. *Sahi nasal hai inki* [They are of a good breed]. Look at that.' He jumps up, eager to show me the pigeon turning a somersault. 'I love them,' declares the otherwise stoic man who takes pride in his masculine prowess. On the floors below, he becomes a landowner who bullies his way through deals, a body builder with a formidable reputation. But here he is a protector and home keeper—a dimension to a man's personality that perhaps even denotes the innate kindness that is bestowed upon every human.

To the kabootarbaaz waiting for his birds on his rooftop, the years of money lost on these birds has not dulled his spirit. Staring at the horizon, he jumps up when he sees a silhouette form, the hope that his bird, now appearing amongst that white patch of clouds, will come back from the unknown nooks and crannies of the world and swerve down into his outstretched hand. Kabootarbaaz and the kabootar—the men with their feet on the earth, looking skyward and hoping for the magic to be recreated, and the others with wings, who have a single purpose: to come back home to their men.

5

THE STORYTELLERS
OF ANDHRA

The oil lamps hanging from the trees are dim, but they still glow like sweet honey on the faces of the audience. Crickets hum in the distance, and a few dogs can be seen dozing near discarded truck tyres. For a while, everything is silent—even the restless bunch of children sitting cross-legged before the tiny stage decorated with marigold flowers. Moments later, a trio, with their indigenous instruments, perched atop the platform, clear their throats, the sensitive microphone turning the sound into a deep reverberating screech. Once silence is restored, they break into song, filling the air with their poems. They tell stories, sometimes all night long—legendary stories that the villagers gather to hear every year around bonfires during the winter months and, sometimes, in the cool evenings of the summer. These are stories that their fathers and grandfathers have heard. Stories that they have heard before and want to hear again. Of lovers, kings, gods and beggars. Stories that dissolve in their bloodstreams like pearls in the sea, becoming tender memories that comfort them like a mother's soft caress. The quest for a lost childhood, after all, is an ancient one.

Kothagadi is small village in Vikarabad in the state of Telangana. Every Sankranthi,[1] women decorate the thresholds of their houses in this town of a few hundred, making wriggly rangoli patterns from rice flour in the wee hours of the morning—a chalky welcome-mat to the most modest of huts. Later in the afternoon, they gather in open courtyards outside their huts and bind together sesame seeds with sugar syrup to make sweet balls of laddus.

Children fly kites in open fields during the day, and in the evening the villagers collect money to bring over our storytellers: the Burrakatha artists from the nearby town in Vikarabad. Burrakatha is an oral tradition that employs poetry and music in an all-night session of storytelling. Those who contribute more to the fund sit on plastic chairs along with the local MLA and the temple priest. The rest make do with sitting on the ground or perching on the thick branches of banyan trees; some, more than others, squat on the blue tarpaulin sheets that have been donated by a charity organization from Hyderabad, to watch the three storytellers shake their heads like the bobblehead dolls of Thanjavur,[2] narrating long tales characterized by wit and quick-fire repartee, their voices like smooth velvet, intoxicating like toddy.

Burrakatha stories, usually mythological, historical and sociopolitical in nature, are the twentieth-century version of what was earlier known as Jangamkatha.[3] The form has been improvised from the original, where the central underlying message was religious, with separate moral codes of conduct for the different strata of society, divided on the basis of class, caste and gender.

The origins of Jangamkatha have an interesting parable attached to them. A long time ago, when the gods and goddesses still lived in the cold, white mountainous paradise well beyond the clouds, the four founding fathers of the Budaga Jangam[4] tribe were walking below them through dense jungles, hunting rats to take home as food. Pitying their desperation, Goddess Parvati requested her all-powerful husband to grant them a better life. The all-knowing Lord Shiva explained that they didn't deserve better. But on his wife's insistence, he suggested the men be tested before deciding their fate. Dressed as earthly beings, Parvati and Shiva appeared before the four men and offered solutions for a better way of life. Unfortunately, instead of honouring the god and goddess, they attempted to rape Parvati, so the infuriated Shiva cursed them in perpetuity to a life as beggars and nomads. And, thus, say the legends, dawned an era of the nomadic storytellers— the *jangam*s, or 'nomads' in Telugu. In the twelfth century, they took up the Virashaivism[5] religion under the influence of its propagator, Basava—a Karnataka-based saint who worshipped Lord Shiva and used the religion to combat caste issues and social inequality. It was a rebellion of sorts. But the religion soon dissipated and the jangams gave up their lifestyle, quickly going back to non-vegetarianism and alcohol. For their livelihood they continued begging and performing Burrakathas, in which they narrated stories of the much-venerated Shiva as well as other tales that they picked up while begging from village to village.

On the makeshift stage, the chief narrator, known as the *kathakudu*, sits in the middle, wearing fitted pyjamas with a loose robe and belt, and a plumed turban that seems to have collected dust, grime and sweat over the years. The fast-paced dialogues have him switching between multiple characters within seconds—one moment he is the vigilant, wise narrator and the next he is mimicking the cagey subtlety of women characters, and an instant later, he becomes the enigmatic, chimerical Lord Shiva. The younger audience lies back, relaxing with hands under their chins. To them, the storytellers seem to have all the innocence of a grandparent recounting tales. The elders have, meanwhile, drawn their knees up to their chins, the narrator's voice flowing like cool, buttery toddy; their sleepy, tired, lolling heads jerk up as the characters come alive.

This endearing art form can seem discordant in less able hands, but the kathakudu handles the narrative carefully, allowing for a performance that maintains the vital tipsiness of the atmosphere. *'Aieee, Gopeshwara Mahadevaheeeeee...'* The kathakudu starts the evening with a devotional song in praise of their Lord Shiva, using a copper ring, an *andelu*, in his right hand for the taal, meaning 'beat'. A *tambura*, the fretless Indian lute, is strung across his shoulder. The tambura provides the origins of the word Burrakatha— the term *burra* refers to the tambura, while *katha* means 'story'. The kathakudu pulls the string of the tambura to a soprano, stretching it to achieve maximum tension, while closing his eyes in concentration.

'Pani, pani, pani . . .' chimes in the *rajkiya*, a young moustachioed man on a *dimki*, a drum made of animal skin stretched over a mud pot, enabling it to produce a

distinctly metallic sound regarded as an indispensable part of the Burrakatha performance. Apart from helping the narrator string the story together, the rajkiya cuts in on the narration with comments on contemporary political and social issues. The drummer to his left, the *hasyam*, meanwhile, cracks jokes throughout the performance with his wit and verve.

'*Dubulu rajyam paripalinchuta . . .*' In the silence of the night the kathakudu begins the story of the king of a village in Andhra. Soon, the tale will be embellished with songs, comments, melodies, tunes and expressions. 'A village in the arid region of the Deccan plateau dries up due to drought,' he recounts to his audience of fifty-odd villagers, the rajkiya stitching the story together with his acknowledgements—'*haan*', '*pani*'.

'The king, queen and their young prince, along with their pet dog, leave the village to find newer pastures.' His hands move to create mountains, jewels, forests, dust and prisons, his voice steadily thickening with a gradual rise in volume, carefully holding back his pitch for a climb to a melodic peak until the very end. 'They travel far and wide, encountering monsters, wise rishis, evil spirits and dangerous animals . . .' There is a brief pause, only to be immediately followed by a chorus from the other two raconteurs. '*Dublugundu tambuda, bajerao tambuda . . .*' the hasyam and the rajkiya croon, the sounds punctuated by beats from their drums, the blur of their knuckles competing with the flapping of a hummingbird's wings.

'The royal family finally arrives at a neighbouring kingdom,' continues the kathakudu as the sounds of the instruments wane, 'hoping someone shows them mercy with some food. But the king of this neighbouring land, Kamleshkota, has other plans. Petty and trite as he is, he challenges the king to a fight.' He builds on the story, increasing his pitch. A frenzied queen, a peppery parrot of a minister along with a sleek wise adviser in Kamleshkota's court join the character list. The kathakudu's rendition alters from agitated to piquant as the characters come alive, like words dancing between the audience and the narrator.

By now, the artists have aroused the curiosity of the audience, all of them wide-eyed in anticipation. The villagers are on their haunches, gaping at the raconteurs whose sparkly vigour conjures up fanciful delights—opening the doorway to their imaginations. 'The challenge is to get his pet pig to fight the visiting king's malnourished pet dog. The visiting king begs and pleads otherwise.'

'"I'm here only to look for some food." Kamleshkota, relishing the power play, refuses to relent. The kathakudu fleshes out the king's character: "Two kings can't live on the same land," roars Kamleshkota.' And the rajkiya chimes in, 'Just like Andhra and Telangana[6] cannot be together,' the line earning a hearty applause from the audience.

'"If my pig wins, you become my slave. If your dog wins, I will leave my throne and make you the king,"' roars the kathakudu, his voice a deep-throated baritone now; he plays the character of the king, his eyes turning into balls of fire as the drums roar louder. The atmosphere is thick with anticipation, and the kathakudu's narration cuts through it deliciously.

The dog ultimately wins in the story and Kamleshkota leaves the kingdom. Peace and prosperity prevail over the village under the new righteous king.

'The gentle bee is singing, is dancing, Tummeda.'[7] The rajkiya and hasyam start singing a celebratory song to their dimkis.

> She announces rain, the gentle bee, Tummeda
> The river with the golden mouth flows, Tummeda
> It ripens all the nine jewels, Tummeda
> The bee in the forest where the honey fills up, Tummeda
> In the fields, the fruits are filled with honey too, Tummeda
> In this way, the farmers happily harvest the crop.

'Kamleshkota ultimately repents his sins and throws himself into a river, flowing away with the fresh water and flowers, learning and unlearning throughout the rest of his life journey.' The kathakudu finishes after about two hours; the account elicits a spontaneous wave of gusto from the audience, encouraging the Burrakatha artists to narrate another story. A few men, tanked up on toddy,[8] dance in wild abandon while their women cheer them on.

'We don't care about the Andhra–Telangana divide,' says the kathakudu as he sips hot chai during the interval, introducing himself as Anjalayya Jangam. 'It is a fight between the kings, politicians. We are simply an audience.

Maku anta saman [For us, everyone is the same].' His voice is a papery rasp, beads of sweat form on his nose and chin and a musty smell fills the air as he sits on the ground beside me. Anjalayya is small, but has a vibrant energy in spite of his age, as if he would never need help getting up after long hours spent sitting.

'In the last few years of united Andhra, we were called by the local activists twice or thrice to perform in villages and narrate stories that create a need for Telangana.' He wipes his wet eyebrows on his sleeve. 'The party leaders gave us the brief and we adapted it to an old Burrakatha,' he drawls, pausing to think; he closes his bloodshot eyes for a few moments to block out the lights from the halogen lamps shining on his face. 'In theatre, there is the fourth wall, whereas in storytelling there is no fourth wall.[9] We sometimes change the pace of the story, and its plot, to suit the audience's reaction. At other performances of the story narrated tonight, we beat up Kamleshkota and have dogs chase him out of the kingdom. But the men in this village are peaceful and avoid clashes. They'd rather not hear about so much blood and gore and so Kamleshkota is penitent instead.'

Anjalayya often innovates while addressing the needs of political parties to take their manifestoes to the voters, adapting the plots to address the problems of the particular village where they are performing. 'In one village, we tapped on the problem of electricity, in another, we tackled water supply. Address these issues in a form, in a format, with which they are familiar, and they will eat out of your hands.' He nods his head.

Back in the early years of Indian independence, when the Telangana People's Movement[10] had first taken shape amongst the peasants to resist the feudal government, Burrakatha changed from being merely a local folk art. It was brought into the mainstream by a popular theatre movement in the 1940s known as the Praja Natya Mandali,[11] and by Marxist poets like Sunkara and Sheikh Nazir, who used this form to generate local activism amongst the backward castes and middle classes.

The wandering artists reached villages where the government was yet to make inroads—simplifying party propaganda using their understanding of village customs, culture and concepts for the largely illiterate voters. The Praja Natya Mandali used this strategy with great effect, adapting the traditional forms used for narrating historical and mythological stories into political narratives to convey the revolutionary message. Although introduced in the Andhra region, the Burrakatha soon became a popular art form in the Telangana movement.

Since Burrakatha was a medium to educate people about the political situation, the British government had banned it in Madras, where the art form had gained momentum during colonial times, and the Nizam's government banned the left-leaning folk art in the princely state of Hyderabad.

'Sunkara Satyanarayana's *Telangana* was also written at that time. We often sang it during the last few years of the revived movement,' says Anjalayya, speaking of the subversive katha, written in 1944, on the heroism of Bandhagi, a Muslim peasant, who fought valiantly against the oppression of the feudal landlord Deshmukh, illustrating that the struggle was not a communal one, but was rather a struggle against oppression. 'Often, these stories caused an emotional upheaval in the audience too. Such was their effect that by the end of the recital, chairs were broken, protests were launched for a separate state immediately, with villagers proceeding in jeeps to the city. My brother was hurt on his head once during the riots after a session. A shard of glass was hurtled in his direction . . .' Anjalayya murmurs, unconsciously clicking the *andelu*s, the hollow brass rings that contain several metal balls that rattle and ring. Within the village economies, the andelus are often fastened to bullock carts to provide a hypnotic *ching, ching, ching* to keep the bullocks pacified, deafening the alarming sounds from their immediate surroundings.

Except for a few, most of the villagers have left for their homes for a quick meal. An organizer stops by to switch off the halogens lighting the stage. Darkness falls. Slowly, one after the other, sounds cease. 'You have about half an hour left before we start another session,' the organizer hastily informs Anjalayya before disappearing into the darkness. Anjalayya clears his throat, gulping down the remains of his tea. 'I have heard that movie singers gargle with honey and clove every morning to keep their voices melodious. We just make do with this ginger tea.' He chuckles, the moonlight shining on the ridges of his brow and eyes while his face and jaw are swallowed up by the darkness. Although this recital of three or four stories will finish around dusk, some long Burrakatha performances may be serialized over several consecutive evenings, sometimes even taking as long as three to four days.

Moving to a darker, quieter corner behind the stage, Anjalayya describes the ingredients of a good tale. 'Now, a short story can never be a good tale. It has . . . no . . . teaching value,' he explains in staccato bursts. 'Epics! Those are great. Our religions, like those of the Hindus and Buddhists, are rooted in beautiful stories. Even Christians have parables on Christ. Those are good stories,' he adds firmly. 'They go back to the past, when men and women crossed rivers, jungles and mountains to get where they had to—with witchcraft, animals, parahumans, gods, heroes and powerful villains. There is no beauty in contemporary tales. Because there is only so much that you can experience from the window of a car, train or a bus. The best stories are the ancient legends and epics,' he reaffirms. 'The people that the characters met through their journey, the perils they encountered, and the problems that were solved along the way.'

Anjalayya, now in his fifties, learnt the craft from his grandparents in his hometown in Mehboobnagar, a few hours from Hyderabad. His parents were too busy travelling around the Telangana and Rayalseema region, narrating epics at the parties of moneyed landlords for festivals like Shivratri. 'Nobody in my family ever went to school. We don't understand letters. But I know at least four epics by heart, which is about one lakh lines in all. *Yellamma*, *Bobbulikatha*, *Kumara Rama Katha*, *Ramayana Katha*,' he says with some perfunctory chest puffing. 'Do you know

Daroji Eerama?' he asks excitedly, disappointed that I hadn't heard of her before. 'She was a legend and could recite at least ten kathas from memory. I wish I could have trained under her,' he adds wistfully. 'Burrakatha artists just know words, amma, words with magic that pierce through the clamour of the world,' he says, surprised at having found a catchy phrase. He smiles, satisfied. He does not know where the phrase came from. He did not know that he had the phrase within him.

'Telling a story is like reading a book without pictures,' he continues. 'My listeners make the scenery, depending on their understanding of a character or a word. For some, the king Kamleshkota looks like the rich businessmen who conned land out of them last year, while to others, he may look like a moustachioed Ranga Rao of *Mayabazar*—that Telugu film of the 1950s.' He laughs.

Anjalayya, along with his brothers-in-law, grew up in the Mehboobnagar of the 1990s, where a highway had emerged complete with a black top, indigenous fauna and wide lanes that functioned as veins to the economically feeble region of Andhra. A housing project evolved, and an English-medium school catered to the region's elite. A few government self-employment schemes were introduced to eradicate poverty, but soon, the power project failed to deliver, and the schemes collapsed. A few of the already rich people in the village became richer, but Anjalayya realized his family only became poorer.

He came to realize others things too. That he was a Budaga Jangam. Like his parents, he too would have to beg for a living. Unlike the other children in school, he never wore socks, and never had handkerchiefs in his pocket, the kind with delicate lace trimmings, which made him wonder why anybody would waste so much time on things with which you wipe your nose. While most children lived in villages, he had to walk for miles because the homes of his people were on the fringes of villages and towns. He realized he was different on the days his parents came back home without performing, when they had to fry lizards and rats to fill their stomachs.

Like most people of his community, Anjalayya could never receive his scheduled caste certificate from the government because he belonged to a migratory tribe with no fixed residential address, depriving him of the benefits available to scheduled caste communities in India.

'Even when we sang songs in praise of the same lord that they prayed to, they never let us into the temples. They laughed when my father attempted to enrol us in high school. '"Since when did lower-caste people start getting educated," they'd jibe,' Anjalayya recounts bitterly.

'My brother and I stole the slippers that the upper-caste Brahmins left outside the temples and threw them away in the river. Silly things; their heads can grow soft with all the time they spend plonked on their beds indoors, with no sun,' he titters nervously. 'They should start hunting rats in the forests too. That'd sharpen them.' And then, as the village headman's wife crosses the path a few metres away from us, he whispers in a guardedly clipped tone, 'We also took quick sips from their cups while they spoke of village politics.' He raises his eyebrows at my surprise, waggling them with speed, and then breaks into hearty laughter.

Anjalayya often uses this gesture with his eyebrows to emote 'paradise' in his performance. According to him, this is also how the otherwise-teetotaller Brahmins would react if they had their first taste of toddy one day. 'It will help them loosen up a bit too.'

'A rich Brahmin landlord hired us to work on his fields long ago. We'd work the ragi fields during the day and sit through long hours of Burrakatha performances in the neighbourhood at night,' he says, stretching his legs before him, massaging the soles of his feet. 'We recited our lines while throwing seeds in the field, practised them as we worked on the rethatching of our huts after the monsoon, and tested each other while climbing trees to pick ripe mangoes.'

Anjalayya, by his late teens, had mastered the kathas and was ready to perform like his parents. He, along with his brother and brother-in-law, performed more than ten kathas a month in Mehboobnagar and the surrounding districts. They performed at weddings, Shivratris and birth and death ceremonies.

'The shorter ones lasted about three hours,' he says, 'and the longer ones lasted all night. We charged five hundred rupees for these kathas. My friend Siriyala, who is from this village, demanded double that amount. *Telivaina vaadu!* He was almost as famous as the renowned Bhakta Siriyala, the great devotee Siriyala, among the people. A film-maker from Madras approached him to record a film song for a Tamil movie, but he only knew Telugu, like us. I wish we had learnt another language. And maybe some new instruments. Like the piano. Or modern drums, maybe. Maybe then we could sing songs for the cinema,' he says, fingering the andelu, which must have been cold to the touch in the midnight air.

The interval had been extended to an hour and a half as the MLA had an important call to attend. The rajkiya and hasyam are now preparing their dimkis for the rest of the performance. Passed on to them by their grandfathers, the dimkis are at least 150 years old. The rajkiya informs me that no one makes them like this any more. 'You need to beat the skin very thin and smooth and stretch it over the pot,' he says, pouring cold water into the open end of the drum, wetting the dried and beaten goat hide drawn over it.

'It makes a thin, soft sound that way,' Anjalayya explains. 'Old wisdom.'

About two decades ago, television started making forays in the Andhra villages; cricket on television and songs on the radio ate into the evening hours of the villagers, leading to a dwindling of the sense of community. 'People used to get together in the evenings to hear stories around fires, sharing food and toddy. These days, they want everything within their four walls. Farmers here don't even share their seeds with one another.' Anjalayya sighs. In the more recent past, musical bands, that sing bhajans and stories and use contemporary instruments and employ marketing teams, have marked the end for Burrakatha artists in the region. About eight years ago, Anjalayya and his brothers migrated from Buranpur, the village where they grew up, in search of better working conditions, leaving behind at least four generations of legacy.

'We settled in another village in Mehboobnagar and sought help from our friends there. A cassette company called Kamala Videos recorded our songs on *Yellama Burrakatha*,' Anjalayya says as he removes his plumed turban to set his hair, the grey bristles on his head as long the ones on his chin. 'But it never sold. We then went to Vikarabad and performed once in a while at Shivratri or death ceremonies. The rest of the time, we helped carry bricks and stone chips at a construction site. My knotty limbs are too old to do manual labour, but my grandchildren work. They earn enough to keep our family of ten eating,' he adds.

'What do they do?' I ask him.

'They are garbage cleaners.' He smiles.

An organizer comes by and, with a grumpy shake of the head, waves at them to begin.

'The villagers are back from their dinner,' he says. We cross a dry creek with wild grass growing in its bed. The country is grey and treeless to my left, and on my right, the acacia trees loom over hills like low hung clouds. This small village grows rice every now and then. There is barely any cattle, and no fences—the countryside is too arid for grazing.

'Change, they say. I knew change was inevitable. I just expected change for the better,' he smiles as they are hurried on by the MLA's secretary to the stage.

'You cannot keep sir waiting. Now rush,' the secretary chides them. Anjalayya and his brothers will now start a performance on the *Bobbulikatha*, the most loved epic of the state, where kings kill men like pieces on a chessboard.

An age-old animosity existed between the houses of Bobbili and Vizianagaram. As a result, many feuds occurred between these two houses, culminating finally in the battle of Bobbili on 24 January 1757. Various reasons exist for these feuds, mainly political, economic and geographical, but some consider caste as the main factor for their enmity. While the rulers of Bobbili were Velamas, the rulers of Vizianagaram were Kshatriyas. According to the Hindu caste system, Kshatriyas are superior to Velamas.

As Anjalayya and company begin, their descriptions evoke a spontaneous wave of enthusiasm from the audience—the pride and valour of the Velama clan; the battle where 250 courageous soldiers of Bobbili were up against the combined forces of more than 10,000 Vizianagaram and French soldiers; and the ploy to kill the king of Vizianagaram. In the end, the brave General of Bobbili commits suicide, rejecting the disgrace of dying at the hands of his enemy, but his stories of glory live on . . .

6

THE STREET DENTISTS
OF BARODA

'*Ek mahine se dard hai* [I have been in pain for a month]!' cries out the old man, opening his mouth to reveal more than a few skewbald teeth, mementos from a zealous cigarette-smoking career. Amrit Singh, sitting on his haunches before him, dips his weathered hands in a bowl of blue liquid and jams a fist into the old man's mouth to feel his gums.

'Oh, *kuch nahi hai bhai* [It is nothing],' Singh says. '*Torus hai*[1] . . . It's just a little extra bone poking your jaws,' he says, wiping his hands on a soiled cloth.

'Can you take it out then?' whimpers the old man.

'We could consider the possibility. But why do you need to?'

'Why not?' the old man persists.

'I don't know,' Singh snaps, suddenly annoyed. 'Why isn't the ant as tall as the elephant? *Chalo, niklo . . . Kuch nahi hai toh tumhara paisa bhi nahi lenge.* [Now leave. Since there is no problem, there will be no charge].'

Singh turns to tell me matter-of-factly: 'If he would have gone to the doctors, they would probably have performed in-house surgery, use lots of fancy terms that would allow him to feel miserable, prescribe him a long list of medicines and turn him into a victim of daylight robbery.' His moustache is oiled and smoothened into place; his red turban looks like it has been tied in a hurry.

Singh's humble office is a tidy, though dusty, street shop outside the iconic structure of MS Baroda University, which was founded by Pratap Singh Gaekwad of Baroda, the last maharaja of the former state of Baroda, in 1949. Beyond the periphery of its walls are wraith-like domes and minarets, and in the looming dusk squats Singh on a cobbled pavement, his tools arranged on a red cloth—a few dentures, blindingly white and intended to dazzle, are displayed along with jars, bottles and a tin box that holds extra dental tools. There's no mortar-and-brick structure, no ritzy chairs, no surgical light-head. He won't give you long names for diseases, and you can drop in when you pass by the shop; patients just pull up a bamboo stool and hope that Singh will boot out any pain from their mouths with his corroded set of pliers.

'Yes, I will fill your tooth. No, cavity does not mean you have ants in your teeth,' he tells a patient.

And then to another, 'You've never had a tooth there? Okay, I'll make you one.'

'No, I only take care of teeth. I do not clean ears.'

Amrit Singh is a street dentist, a far cry from his peers at the department of dentistry in the university looming right behind us; men who perhaps toiled on cadavers and practised by giving each other injections. Instead, he was trained by his father, Gurbachan Mehel Singh Digpal, who himself was a street dentist and had blandished his son to join him while Amrit worked at a car garage. '*Pitaji* told me that the work is not that challenging. Almost like fixing punctures and cleaning carburettors,' he jests, oddly sanguine, snorting every time he finds something amusing.

Dentistry as a practice often surfaces in the everyday history of the Indian subcontinent. The Indus Valley civilization has yielded evidence of dentistry being practised as far back as 7000 BC. Explorers at Mehrgarh, Pakistan, in 2006, reported that eleven drilled molar crowns from nine adults were discovered in a Neolithic graveyard in Pakistan dating from 7500–9000 years ago.[2] Skilled beads craftsmen perhaps doubled up as dentists, curing tooth-related disorders by using their tools of trade—bow drills—on teeth.

During the Middle Ages, when vocations were still not cleanly divided into branches, barbers took care of the most ordinary dental needs such as cleaning and whitening. Other extraordinary procedures like tooth extractions, where the gum was often mistakenly removed along with the tooth, were performed by more skilled men such as blacksmiths—their preferred tools of the trade being door keys or forceps. Dentistry, thus, as a profession, was largely unregulated until the twentieth century. The street dentists in modern India, however, mostly learned their skills from the Chinese,[3] who came looking for work in India in the early 1900s. Many of them left China immediately after civil war broke out in the late 1920s and they were being forcefully drafted into the army. Religious India beckoned them, and one of the many communities that came via

Bhutan and Tibet were the Hubei, from a province in central China, where most of the denizens were skilled in the art of dentistry, just as the Hakkas were known for their noodle-making skills. They passed on their expertise to fellow Indians, eager to carve a home among them, teaching them basic dentistry with amalgam fillings for a carious tooth, making dentures and using indigenous materials for the reconstruction of anterior teeth.

Amrit Singh's grandfather learnt his skills in Aara Zilla, near Patna, from a young member of the Hubei community who had wandered away from his flock in the 1920s, struggling to find employment in a nation that was fighting for an independent identity.

'See, that's him,' Amrit Singh says, pulling out a grainy black-and-white tintype photograph of a full-bodied young sardar on to a recycled biscuit jar. *Dadaji ne jawaani ke hisaab se kaam sikh liya* [My grandfather learnt the trade to earn quickly as he was young],' he tells me. 'But there was no work in Bihar. The number of travellers and migrants dwindled with time. So he travelled with his family to Delhi and set up shop near Thandi Sadak in Chandini Chowk with the help of his friend,' he says, scratching the rust off the tin photograph with his thumbnail.

'I was born in Delhi,' he smiles. 'There was great respect for their work because doctors were few back then. They worked through the day, tending to migrants, labourers and their families. We visited people at their homes and often catered to refugees and families who had made their home in what was known as Ahmad Ka Mohalla,[4] then an upmarket neighbourhood for migrants in Chandini Chowk. *Areey yeh clinic wale dentist ab aye hain* [Dentists in clinics have just recently come to the fore]. We have serviced the nation for a much longer time. Ask your grandfather, he will tell you . . . There were thousands of us—in Amarnath, Ahmedabad, Delhi,' he says exuberantly.

Things started changing after Independence, when the Indian Constitution introduced regulations for dentistry practices, requiring dentists, dental mechanics and dental hygienists to be licensed compulsorily, thereby making street dentistry illegal. But dental street practitioners continued to thrive in the dark underbelly of the country.

The Dental Council of India, a statutory body that regulates the profession, says it has no current figures for the number of street dentists in the country, but they are estimated to be under a thousand in number, spread throughout the country.

'Often, people place more trust in us than in doctors . . .' Singh continues.

I must have looked surprised or unconvinced because he stops and explains what he means in the simplest of terms. 'See, your teeth and mouth act like a mirror for the rest of the body. If your stomach is upset, your teeth will have more plaque. If you have acidity, the insides of your teeth will corrode,' he reasons with me.

'We know all this from our years of experience, and we inform our patients accordingly, if required. That's why people trust us. The clinic-wallah dentists have machines for everything. Look at my dentures, I make everything by hand.' He snorts again, proudly lifting a set from the display, tapping the teeth with his greasy, gold-ringed knuckles, to prove their strength. 'I make fix, floating, bridge everything . . . If you want a cover for your teeth, I have them in chrome, gold, silver,' he rattles off a list, counting on his fingers.

'But don't you wish you had those kinds of machines and that education?'

'No,' he says, his face falling. He pauses. For a moment Singh loses his sanguinity, but he checks himself. '*Ohho*, what is the point? Everyone has their speciality. I do this for poor people who cannot afford other dentists. I don't take care of root canals, swollen gums or bleeding gums. Those the doctors do. I do dentures, tooth replacement, cleaning . . . All cheap and of good quality.' He touches his index finger to his thumb to make an 'okay' sign. 'My relations are very good. People come to me from villages all around Baroda, sometimes from Mumbai and Ahmedabad too.'

Singh gets his acrylic resin and porcelain for making dentures from 'Dinesh Bhai who lives off Sayajiganj near the World Trade Centre in Baroda'. Although the wires may sometimes leave a metallic taste in the mouth, they work out to be most durable and cheap, he reveals. Holding a saddle-shaped mould made of chromium wires between his legs, he pours the resin. The occasional fly alights on his hands, the instruments and the patients. Still, there is an element of savoir faire about the archaic craft. The colour and size of the dentures depend on the patient's mouth size, shape, skull size, age, sex, skin colour and hair colour. 'You know all this from experience. A fair person can't have very white teeth. They need that yellow tinge.'

'I'll tell you one more thing. You can make a person look younger by giving him longer teeth,' he winks. 'It's a trick of the trade. Thirty years in the business will teach you this. My wife tells me that I'm like a thief, I never look anyone in the eye. I am always looking at their mouths instead—mentally rebuilding them.' He laughs, snorting a few times in between, chattering incessantly as dentists do.

'How many days do you take to finish a pair of dentures?' I ask him.

'The clinic-wallah dentist takes some ten days to make it, but we finish the job in a few hours,' he says, chest puffing up a bit as he picks at an imaginary thread on his forearm.

Licensed dentists use wax to make a preliminary impression of the patient's mouth and then make a diagnostic cast. Once an appropriate preliminary cast has been obtained, the final mould is made using gypsum, a stone-like product. This final shape is inspected, customized and approved before being used to manufacture the teeth.[5]

'I make mine on a *bhatti*, or on a furnace, with acrylic resin in one straight go.'

'Is there no need to test with samples before that?'

'Humph!' he grunts at me. 'Now now, you have spoken like someone with deep pockets,' he mocks. 'There's no need to make so many casts. Poor people can't spare so much time, *ji*; they need everything fast and cheap.'

Singh continues, 'Now, do you see this guy coming?' He points to a small, feeble man crossing the road in a grey uniform. 'He is Radhe, a peon at an office in Sayajiganj, and he has been losing a tooth every other month for the past year,' Singh explains, opening his wooden box that contains teeth of all sizes, shapes and shades. His bridges—false teeth that are permanently fixed to the teeth on either side of the gap using a special cement—are unequally shaped, stocky and carefully painted to match each other.

Radhe squats on the stool before Singh, pulls a tattered book out of his wallet and starts reciting the Hanuman Chalisa, a devotional hymn addressed to Lord Hanuman—the god with the repository of incomparable strength—chewing his sloppy lips as he flips through the pages. 'I have been brushing thrice a day now,' he announces after finishing the hymn, hoping for some approval—'You're being very disciplined!'—but, instead, Singh says, 'Oh, there's no need to do that.'

It turns out Radhe hasn't been able to afford dental care his whole life, and when one of his front teeth started rotting, a masonry worker pulled it out with a set of pliers. 'It's much better just to get it out of there. The space that the tooth leaves behind fills on its own anyway. Although, I smile less often these days,' Radhe tells me, his nervous laughter dying in his throat as Singh randomly starts picking the 'right tooth' from the box.

'But now I can't eat much. I have a lower-paying job and my wife screams at me when she has to make separate meals for our four children and me. So I have to come to Singhji *daantwale*,' he says, opening his mouth wider to reveal a few missing teeth, his pumpkin-shaped head and the gaps between his teeth making him look like a scarecrow being victimised by pesky birds. He nervously plays with the lace of his shoe, a toe peeking in and out of a hole, like a jittery animal. Teeth-wise, Singh has brought him back from hell, he claims. In the course of their two-year relationship, he has removed two of his lower incisors and a canine, cemented in place two posts and filled two cavities.

'How long do these products last,' I ask Singh, noticing a chip in the tooth that he is fixing for Radhe. 'Easily five to eight years,' he replies, smoothing the tooth with a file-like tool. 'Indians have much better teeth because we eat hard substances all the time, unlike foreign people. A dentist from Scotland told me this when she visited me after hearing about "our kind" from a tourist.' He laughs, putting aside his tools to show a postcard from her with a blue Queen Elizabeth stamp, dated March 2001. 'It was nice meeting you,' he reads out the card before carefully putting it back in his bag.

'Tooth decline begins typically when fragments of food get stuck between the teeth,' Singh explains while putting Radhe's bridge in his mouth with his bare hands. Radhe is perspiring profusely; the sweat on his forehead soon starts trickling down to his throat. 'This Radhe,' he says, tugging at his bridge a little more forcefully than required, making Radhe jerk in pain, 'refuses to stop eating *kheni*.'[6] He gives the patient a cold stare. 'The food rots and a cavity begins to blossom, reaching the pulp tissue and creating that insistent throbbing. The tooth turns brown and then I scoop out the cavity. But he comes to me after that. Now, you might assume he can crack open walnuts with his teeth. But no,' Singh says as he inserts the bridge in Radhe's mouth, squinting as the sun sets and disappears behind the domes of the university, leaving an orange-and-pink sky behind.

'There is a lot more work left to be done on his teeth. But we'll deal with it some other day.'

Because the teeth have to be positioned exactly on top of each other, the setting has to be perfect, so Singh puts the bridge in and then removes it to make some modifications. He twists and turns the teeth in their position, over and over again. *'Theek hai?* [Okay?]' Singh asks the peon. Radhe makes a sound acknowledging him—*'Ae-oo'*. There is no swig of whisky to relieve his pain; there is no biting of a bullet here.

The air is punctuated alternately with *'Theek hai'* and *'Ae-oo.'*

After Radhe lunges back desperately, almost tumbling off his stool, Singh snaps, 'What?'

'Can we stop for two minutes?' Radhe mumbles, his mouth filled with saliva. 'It's hurting.'

'Who asked you to eat kheni then?'

'Chalo, ek aur daant kal hoga [The next tooth we will fix tomorrow],' Amar informs his patient after about fifteen minutes. Radhe barely stretches his bloody mouth to whimper, and then signals me to move so that he can use a sand-filled

spittoon installed by the university. He gargles with the water he carries in a plastic bottle in his bag, spits again, this time on a fenced tree, and then hands over a wad of ten-rupee notes to Singh and wanders away down the road.

'See, I charge very less.' Singh touches the money to his head, thanking his god for his daily bread, before putting it in his shirt pocket. 'About fifty to sixty rupees for a bridge. And hundred rupees for a tooth. So for an entire denture of twenty-eight teeth, that would be about 2800,' he rattles off, like a hawker selling fish in the market.

'But some patients give me 2000 rupees and some 2200, depending on what they can afford. This amount for a set of dentures is the least possible, these days. Even colleges set up by the trusts charge that much. In Pipariya, at Manubhai Dental College and even at Jalaram, they charge this much. But, of course, they are not as quick with their service,' he says with the feline cynicism with which he eyes a 'colleague's' handiwork.

'Ten years ago, I used to see twelve or thirteen patients a day. Now we have just five or six complaining of feeling mildly uncomfortable, say, a cavity or a totally avulsed tooth. *Ab roj toh choksi ka kaam nahi hota haina* [It isn't every day that I work on dentures, after all].' He nods his head regretfully.

'So I earn around 500 rupees,' he says. 'Dental clinics and hospitals are everywhere these days. It is becoming difficult with all the fancy advertising they do.' Singh snorts, folding his legs beneath him, wriggling his toes to avoid a case of the pins and needles.

By now the sun has almost vanished and the domes of the university make a frieze of amber against an opal sky. The evening lamps have been switched on by the municipal corporation. Singh starts packing his things one by one, closing his tooth box, putting all the rusty pliers in, screwing the bottle caps on. Further down the pavement, a group of students in their lab coats gather under a peepul tree and buy cigarettes and mint gum from a tobacco shop. Singh's neighbour, a fakir who sells semi-precious stones and *tabiz*es brings us hot cups of chai. '*Aaj jaldi chutti ho gayi inki* [They got off early today],' the fakir points out to Singh.

'*Haan*, they start their holidays today,' replies Singh, eyeing the students over the rim of his plastic cup.

'Their fourth year will start in a month.' he laughs and then turns to me. 'When could I have ever found so much time to study? I have a family of six to feed,' he says, shaking his head.

When he has no customers, Singh often engages in 'timepass' activities with the fakir and the watchman at one of the university gates.

'Have they ever raised an objection to you practising here?' I ask Singh. To other people, who, like Singh, work in the skulking shadows of the cities where their jobs are considered illegal, this could have been a repulsive question. But to him, I was being hysterical. 'No,' he guffaws, putting his cup of tea aside until his laughter subsides. 'Why would you say that? I'm a *pak-saaf* person, *haina*, Syed?' He turns to a fiercely nodding Syed.

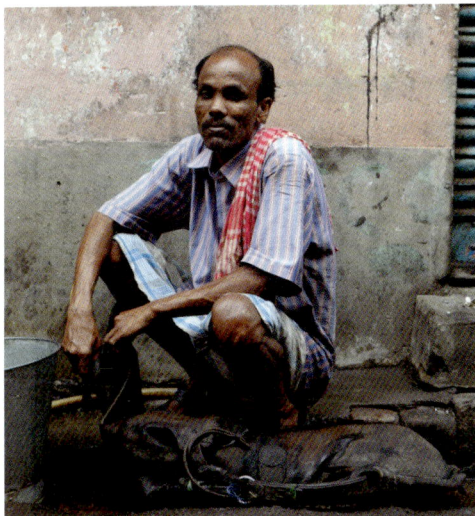

A *bhisti* wallah filling water from a handpump in
Bow Barracks, Calcutta

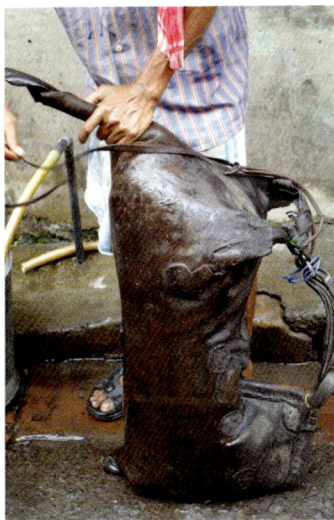

The bhisti wallah's *mashq*—a water bag made
from goatskin

A boat maker working on a boat's carcass in Balagarh, Hooghly district, West Bengal

A boat maker giving finishing touches to a boat in Rajbanshi *para*, Balagarh, West Bengal

Wasim Ahmed, a calligrapher, teaching his students at the Urdu Academy, New Delhi

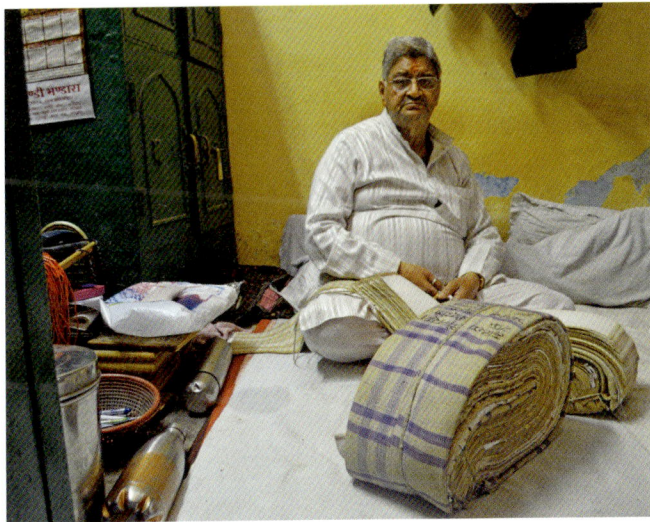

Genealogist Mahendra Kumar Panda in his office in Haridwar

Genealogist Mahendra Kumar Panda scans through the ancient records known as *vahi*s

Nowri Tikri from Jharkhand displays an array of Godna tattoos on her forearm

Syed Abdul Gaffar, an *ittar* wallah from the Old City, Hyderabad, helps a customer sample his handmade ittar

Anil Sood holds a pigeon of the Rekta breed from his prized collection in Old Delhi

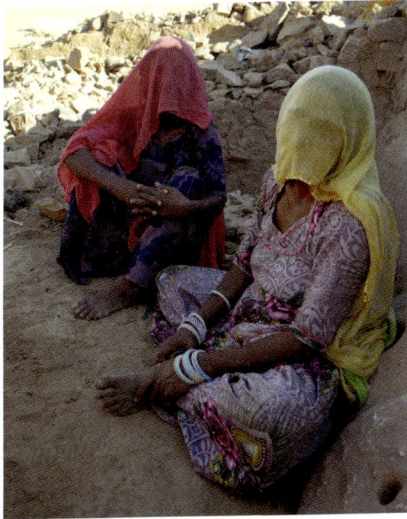

*Rudaali*s Madami and Feroja outside their
dwelling near Jaisalmer, Rajasthan

Anjalayya Jangam, a Burrakatha artist, second from left, with the rest
of his troop near Vikarabad, Telangana

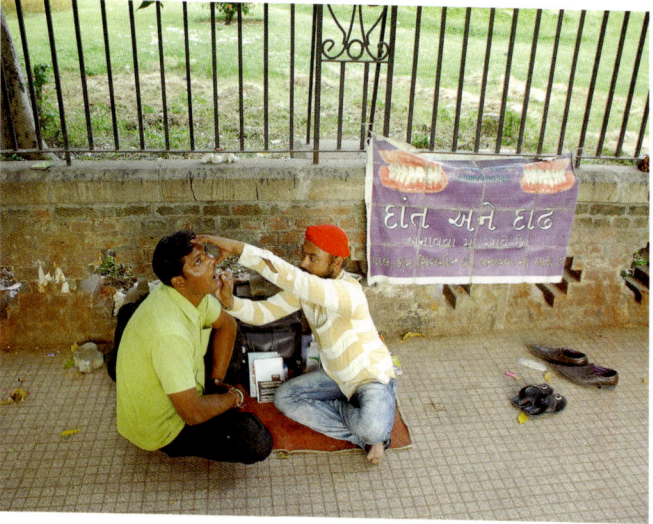

Amrit Singh, a street dentist, fixes the teeth
of his customer in Baroda, Gujarat

A letter writer in Bombay

'These university people don't care as long as we aren't around on big days when national or international dignitaries are meant to arrive,' he says, crushing the plastic cup before throwing it near the pavement.

Street dentists can be a source of embarrassment for a country trying to develop a world-class medical tourism industry,[7] where an estimated 1,50,000 people travel to India for healthcare procedures every year. The Gujarat government, anxious to clear the pavements as part of a clean-up drive to attract more tourists to the state, is cracking down harder than most. The last decade has seen a surge in qualified dentists. Along with the crackdown, this is making it hard for these street practitioners to make a living. Mumbling under his breath, Singh gathers his things and takes our leave, stopping every now and then to buttonhole the chai wallah or a passing student for a quick conversation, until he disappears into the horizon.

Dr Yash R. Patel, an orthodontist based out of Baroda, has seen Singh and his late father all through his growing-up years in India. 'They practise out in the open. It is definitely against the protocol of the dental fraternity in India,' says Dr Patel. 'The lack of hygiene, absence of post-procedure care, the multiple use of instruments and virtually no sterilization exposes the patients to infection. Also, they don't really create a new set of dentures, they just fix the ones they have and adjust them around,' he explains.

'I understand their existence, given the fact that there were very few qualified dentists around till a decade ago.

Even Paris had hundreds of unregistered street practitioners till a few years back,' he observes. He is referring to a case where the police smashed a ring of twenty-three fake Syrian dentists[8] operating out of cafes with battery-run drills. The ring served a mainly immigrant clientele. 'Even within the Indian dental fraternity, there are so many bachelor of dental surgery [BDS] doctors performing tooth implants, which is a legally punishable offence,'[9] he says.

'So why aren't they taken under scrutiny,' I ask him.

'They do it in the shadows, at reduced prices, and it is hard to arrest them because this is India. There are few complaints, many beneficiaries and too many loopholes in the law.'

Even though there are more than 180 dental colleges in India that roll out about 13,000 dentists a year, there continues to be a shortage of competent professionals, creating an opportunity for proletarians and quacks. Street dentists, who mostly sit in the busy lanes of Baroda, Varanasi, Delhi and Amarnath, cater to a large section of our Indian society for whom dental care is not only imaginably expensive but, often, inaccessible too. The busy pilgrimage destinations of the Hindu community are the perfect places for street dentists to set up shop for quick treatments.

'But there is no excuse any more,' Dr Patel points out. 'I understand that dental procedures can be expensive in private clinics and hospitals, but government hospitals like Shree R.C. Gandhi Public Dental Hospital provides basic dentures for as cheap as a thousand rupees!' he exclaims.

On my second day in Baroda, I go back to Sayajiganj, walking along the pavement around the gigantic structure of Baroda University. It is still pretty early in the day. The night watchman is cleaning his teeth with a neem stick. A truck, laden with chairs, arrives at the gate and this is when I notice that the university looks a bit more dressed up than the day before. There is a banner at the entrance announcing: 'Graduation Ceremony'. Posters of clubs and student unions have sprung up around the gate. I rest against the wall where Singh sits, hoping that the tea vendor arrives soon with my morning cuppa. Syed the fakir arrives with his paraphernalia before the others do. '*Kaise ho* [How are you]?' he smiles, his forehead wrinkling beneath his skullcap.

'Waiting for Singh *daantwala*?' he inquires.

'Yes, isn't he late today?'

'He should have been here by now. Or he may not come at all today; he must have been tipped off by informers of higher police security today because of the VIPs visiting the college. Come, sit,' he hands me a tattered old Kutch embroidered mat to sit on.

'For how long have you known Amrit Singh?' I ask.

'I have seen him learn the trade. His father died just a few years ago—three years. I think. He can do everything his father did. *Masala acha bharta hai . . . kabhi, kabhi* tablet *bhi deta hai* [He fills cavities and sometimes prescribes tablets too],' Syed says.

'Has he ever been caught by the police?'

'Arré, no. All these things can be a bit exaggerated. This thin fellow from the municipal authority takes a thousand rupees a month as a bribe from him,' he whispers, leaning in.

'That must cut into his already thin margins,' I remark.

'Haan. But he is doing well. Recently, he shifted with his family from a room in Tarsali to a flat in Aslam Quarter,' he says, shrugging his shoulders.

'With his own earnings?'

'Arré, no. Some ministers gave him a flat before the elections last year. *Sardar hai na*, so he was favoured. The government promised to give me one, too, but it never happened,' he laments.

A lady in her forties waddles towards us, balancing grocery bags in both hands. 'Where is Singhji daantwale?' she asks Syed.

'Don't know. Maybe he won't come at all today.'

'*Kyon, raid pad gayi hai kya?* [Has the police raided his stall?] she sniggers, before walking away.

'Wretched woman. She is so ungrateful,' Syed murmurs under his breath. 'The trust hospital left her hanging for an appointment for a month. Her cavity was hurting her and Singh finished the job,' he retorts. 'See, I know what he does is illegal. He has had cases that have gone badly too. But someone has to take care of the poor, right? Where will people like me go?'

I ask him if trusted the hospitals that offered cheap treatment.

'Have you seen the queues there? It takes three or four days and hours and hours of waiting for one set of dentures,' he replies.

'We are daily-wage workers. How will we survive?' His face darkens. 'Or should we keep our mouths closed because our teeth are rotting? Or simply become addicts who resort to more tobacco and kheni and to escape the pain?

'I have seen so many people go down that route. With bad teeth, getting a job can also be a problem.' Bad teeth, according to him, is a sign of limited intelligence, an apparent marker of class. 'They won't give you jobs as maidservants for children, or in hotels and salons. You will be placed in the background somewhere, far from the everyday public eye. That is what happened to Radhe as well. He had a well-paying job as a peon in a private school until his teeth started rotting—and that screeched "poverty" louder than his broken shoes.'

7

THE URDU SCRIBES
OF DELHI

Kashmere Gate is one of the oldest and most thickly populated areas of Delhi. Every square foot here is claimed by someone—hawkers, squatters, beggars asleep on the sidewalks. A street barber, opening his counter across the road, points to a nook in the walls of what was once Shahjahanabad:[1] 'This is where we slept last night,' he says of his door-less home under the starless sky.

This labyrinth of slimy alleys also houses butchers' shops selling goats and fishmongers calling your attention to their freshwater trout. Cyclists move past them, coming precariously close to impact and the near-tumbling of goods from the stalls. Old men hobble back home, their hands laden with vegetable bags, a post-retirement duty bestowed on them by their wives. Hindus, Muslims, Sikhs, all cultures converge here. The main roads run through residential blocks where thousands of humans, animals and vehicles are caught in an endless crusade every hour, negotiating their space in this colossal street theatre.

In the midst of all this, a group of young students, with scraggly beards, spotless white salwars and skullcaps, stride every day through the grimy layers of time—with each step they clamber up a steep incline to shut out this chaos. Each step takes them towards a lime-washed building at the end of the street, wondrously quiet beyond its wrought-iron gate.

This pillared pavilion is the Urdu Academy maintained by the Delhi government, an institution for Urdu-language promotion and teaching, the conserving of history that was long left to turn mouldy by the purveyors of time. The range of books and research published by them is indicative of the academy's journey from humble beginnings to a measure of monetary but—more importantly—literary success.

To the rear of this cultural preservatory of sorts is an oval-shaped room with high ceilings and a solitary window that allows the sunlight to trickle in. The rest of the chamber has adjusted itself to this window—the walls accepting the habits of weather through the days, learning to eliminate all but the sounds of the sparrows. In a darker corner of the room, a large form—that could be merely a dusk-time shadow—lies very still. Perhaps it is an old piece of furniture covered in white, or a marble statue. My eyes adjust to the light in the room and the shadow turns into a figure, a lean man in a skullcap, with smooth, dark tendrils of smoke for a beard, sitting on his knees, finishing his afternoon prayers. Each of his ageing but firm limbs move like they are choreographed—hands, legs and neck working in a practised fashion as he rolls the mat and adjusts his skullcap. There is no extra flutter, twitch or stretch; each movement has a purpose and no superfluous energy goes to waste. Only his neck moves as he reaches to turn on a switch, bathing himself and the room in white light, revealing the walls crammed with verses in Arabic script—billowing and drooping like waves in their wooden frames, all fashioned by him and his students.

He is a *katib*, a scribe and teacher of Urdu, Persian and Arabic calligraphy for over thirty years. In the packed precincts of this room, Wasim Ahmed teaches students his craft, and he works and lives to tell a saga—both story and history muddled into one.

A few handwritten posters with verses from the Koran lie beside him; the flowy, bold lettering in navy and turquoise resembling a watery paradise of rivers and springs, a paradise of a religion that emerged from the land of deserts. I caress it, admiring the lettering, when Wasim turns to me, drawing the posters away. 'Try not to touch these posters.' He frowns. 'The depiction of faces and humans is not permissible in Islam. Instead of pictures, these verses are akin to God for us,'[2] he explains, forcing a smile. 'I am *pak-saaf*. I have washed and performed all the rituals of purification. I can touch them, but being a non-Muslim, you may not have followed the ritual purification,' he says, clearing his throat, his voice somewhat tortured, like a pebble-grinding machine at work.

With a brief smile, he brushes imaginary dust off the posters with his slim, ringed fingers. A pregnant silence fills the room in spite of the old fan whipping through the thick, dry air, the annoyingly happy sparrows chirruping outside and the exaggerated sounds of the sheets of paper as he wastes long minutes rolling each of them.

Moments later, the door to the room opens and a peon brings in two cups of tea. Wasim habitually lifts the cup and holds it against the tube-light to make sure the peon has cleaned it well, snubbing him for the delay in service. 'You are late as usual. I was done with namaz ten minutes ago,' he hisses at him. 'I draw these for some *shaukeen* men in the Diwani[3] style of calligraphy,' he says and finally sighs, turning a little towards me, but only talking in my general direction. 'This style,' he says, pointing to a framed verse hung above his head, 'was the secret official script of the ancient Ottoman courts, and each artist had a distinct style, so much so that it could rarely be forged by someone else.' The letters are intertwined like the threads on a delicate crochet scarf, both flawless in terms of fine design as well flawed in the slight caprices of the artist's hand. 'Each piece can take months to finish,' he continues, 'and many good, devout Muslims display them in their shops and homes. They believe that the sacred verses will bring good vibes and luck. Beautiful calligraphy always celebrates the sounds and meaning of this sacred text.'

'Do you scribe copies of the Koran as well?' I ask.

'The Koran, even a trained katib like me cannot scribe.' He frowns, shaking his head at my ignorance. 'The Koran is inscribed by *huffaz*, people who've learnt the Koran by rote.' They are often checked and certified by government bodies in many countries like Saudi Arabia and Iraq. 'Mostly, I copy educational books and novels that are written by others,' he explains.

'But you are still an artist,' I remark and he looks up with beady-eyed interest, as if the word conjures up the image of an enigmatic, gifted, revered genius.

'Yes,' he says after a long pause, dropping his eyes to a bottle of ink lying before him. 'I'm like an artist and this is art. There is instant reward with this work. You see the result as you move along the paper. Like painting figures on a canvas, these fine arts occur when you are alone—if not always, not always, but . . . I mean . . .' he grumbles, cursing his ageing memory that whisks words off his tongue. Closing his eyes, he searches for the right phrase, his skullcap moving up to reveal his orange hair that, at certain angles, appears to glimmer, as though fired by the thoughts in his brain.

'Sometimes, weeks, months or even years later, I smile, thinking about certain words from Allah that I scribed many eternities ago. And that thought gets my heart beating rapidly,' he says, his deep voice clearer and filled with love for his Allah, like the voice that calls out the morning azan from the dargah. 'It is like being close to Allah.'

The door swings open again, interrupting Wasim's thoughts, and he scowls in response. Twelve students walk into the room, their heads bowed; they cast a quick glance at us before flipping up the backs of their kurtas, so as not to dirty them, and sit up against the wall and hastily start their prayers before class. Wasim glowers again, as if their presence has made it difficult for him to remember things. He lifts his upper lip and flares his nostrils, a grimace that the students have learned to recognize as ominous.

Reputed to be a martinet or, at his benign best, an academic version of Aunt Polly from *Tom Sawyer*, Wasim has a smile that never reaches his eyes. He is an unyielding master of the script and the bane of those with poor handwriting. His mandate: To evolve from block-lettering to graceful, flowing lines and turn illegible Urdu and Arabic doodles into calligraphy. 'Round and then curve. Move your fingers carefully!' he snaps at a student who approaches him with his corrections. 'Did you practise at home?'

'No, *huzoor*,' the student meekly replies, hanging his head.

'This art needs your brain and heart to work together. Work harder, you get that?' he roars, tapping the desk with his knuckles, eyebrows furrowing in a serious rictus.

'*Ji*, huzoor.'

'Can't you say anything else?'

'Huzoor?'

'Off you go,' Wasim shakes his head, scowling, 'and make sure you write that line ten times.' And then, clicking his tongue, he mutters, 'We rely on them to take our traditions forward. Deplorable!' He suddenly thunders, 'These students ask me why Urdu is written from right to left unlike English.' A student or two peer above their boards, suddenly interested in the conversation.

'Now, how do you answer questions like that? Such dimwits. Why are humans born? Why are they being rebuilt in labs? Why repeat God's mistake?' He throws back his head and cackles with laughter.

'Arré , different cultures prescribe different things. The Japanese write in columns, from the top to the bottom. The Greek write from the left to the right. There is nothing wrong in anything, I say. Nothing is wrong with change either,' he continues, softening his voice, but the smile on his face disappears. 'Let us not fight over our differences. Let us not fight for hate. But fighting for discipline, to maintain heritage and culture, can be good sometimes. Just like jihad. If there is something wrong happening, it has to be addressed . . .' he says, closing his fist, turning to address his students, who stare back at him, perhaps wondering if this conversation was still about *khushkhati*.

For a while, everything is silent except for the pleasurable, scratching sound of the reed pens on paper. 'It is a difficult art,' Wasim finally murmurs, as the students start practising Urdu alphabets—alif, *bay*, *pay*—letters neatly piled on top of one another, some dotted with diamonds, most in scripts dating back several centuries. 'It requires training in history and mathematics at the same time. One needs to be aesthetically aware, too—a connoisseur of beauty. But, most importantly, be physically fit for this profession.'

Gauging my surprise at the mention of physical fitness, he explains, 'Yes, a strong spine and back are required. This isn't one of those graphic design classes where with a few clicks here and there, the pages are ready. We put in long hours in this work while maintaining body posture and balance. The hand is aligned with the leg and body in a way so as to cause minimum stress and maximum longevity. No motion of the body should be wasted. Only then can we create a verse in a more poignant form. But not many people can continue *khushnavisi* for long—it strains their lower backs and necks; spondylitis and chronic back pain are common issues for us,' he says, hawk eyes on the students throughout.

'I'm usually nailed to my seat till the late evenings,' he says. 'Every morning, I start promptly after the Fajr prayers, stopping only for lunch.' He then works meticulously until dinner, scribing legions of books—about twenty pages a day in the same font—balanced and exact. 'At least eight or nine years of daily practise is needed to master basic scripts like the Nasta'līq[4]. Add another decade to learn the fancier ones.'

Wasim grew up mostly in Bijnor, Uttar Pradesh, a few hours from Meerut. It was while playing with his friends one day in his early teens that he noticed a mullah making a poster. The mullah was inscribing tiny verses with his hand within the drawing of a figure; painting dark, thick letters within swerving lines to create a verse that finally looked like a Sufi singer with long robes; moving round and round in a trance, seeking pleasure in Allah. Within a few days, he took an apprenticeship under Ustad Khaliq Tonki, an eminent katib. 'It was magical to see the ink flow from the reed pen and catch the paper, an art that brought me close to God. I never thought that was possible . . .' he says slowly. Slow enough for me to imagine the pleasure he felt looking at the drying ink on the paper, like the blood drying on the shiny backs of bare-bodied men on the holy days of Muharram.

'There was also a lot of demand back in my apprenticeship years to write texts from the Koran. It was an honourable deed, for the protection and proliferation of the word of God,' he reminisces. 'This would be a great profession, I thought to myself.' The ustad lived a few villages away and Wasim covered ground every day on foot as well as by hitching rides on the bullock carts of local farmers to reach his teacher's home. This prosaic rhythm of the initial years of labour formed his character—no-nonsense, clear and straightforward. The ustad's daily plodding and lack of sympathy for mistakes, Wasim tells me, became the foundational essence of his own character. He treated himself like the author of books, giving his work the same nurturing care.

Soon, he moved to Delhi looking for work. The vagaries of life were many here, he intrinsically seemed to recognize, so while his writing reveals meticulousness, it is cloaked in light, easy patterns—inspired by everyday Muslim household items like prayer mats, arabesque designs on ink bottles, embroidery on skullcaps, *tasbeeh*, the qiblah compass and diacritic dots and accents. He sat at a window in his home, often looking up the pages and staring through the window and listening to the sounds outside, as writers mostly do.

'Customarily, a teacher never charges a disciple for this pious art. The ustad only expected discipline and loyalty from his students; he took me under his wing after a long testing period, putting to trial my dedication by making me work long hours. We read through many manuscripts with various styles of Khat that were predominant centuries ago. He taught me well and, even now, when an ancient script is brought to me, I can roughly conclude its age,' he says.

It took many hours of sun and cold, and four years of intense practice, for Wasim to learn calligraphy and its myriad forms—Khat-i-Noori, Nasta'līq, Solas, Diwani and Naskh. 'Thirty years later, I'm still trying to master the craft. The only way you are respected in this profession is if you are the best.'

The journey of Islamic calligraphy in the subcontinent is enthralling, making swift progress over time. Calligraphy is essentially pre-Islamic, but, in India, it saw massive development during the Islamic period. Intricately laced with religious or devotional art during the initial years, it was mostly used to draw the suras from the Koran and then later adapted to different texts. In the beginning of the sixth century, the reign of the Ghorids—a medieval Islamic dynasty of the eastern Iranian lands—in India saw books such as *Tarikh-i-Fakhr-i-Mudabbir* and *Fawaid-ul-Fawad* in floriated Kufic.[5] The Mughal rule from the tenth to the eighteenth centuries gave way to the golden period of calligraphy in the subcontinent, developing styles such as Nasta'līq, Rayhan, Reqa and Sekasta. Due to a higher rate of literacy among the nobility, calligraphy became a pastime for everyone with means.

'I wrote the text for schoolbooks for the state board in Kashmir,' recalls Wasim, speaking of his early years of work. 'I absorbed all the knowledge in my isolation—studying geography, which I never did in my own school. Then there were the *Mughal Shehzadiyan*, a book on the lives and literary contributions of Mughal princesses. There was lots of literature on *shayari* too. And that children's paperback . . . what was it called . . .' He strains his weary eyes trying to recollect silhouettes from the vast vista of his work.

Drawing back, he carefully takes out a large box of mysterious handwritten papers and books from the wooden chest he writes on—ranging from material on mushairas to school texts to religious books—assembled into hand-sewn books or wrapped in advertising fliers, newspapers and crumpled gift wrappers. 'Ah, here it is, *Subah Ki Pari.*' He points to a frail book with yellowing paper. 'What a beautiful book! They don't write them like this any more.' The pages have text neatly printed in black—sometimes floral or plaited, making bold and beautiful handwritten art on paper—but there is not a single drop of ink or a stray line anywhere. 'I have written countless books in Urdu and hundreds in Arabic, and they really paid me for learning from them,' Wasim says, chuckling excitedly, hardly able to maintain his usual composure.

Back in the Mughal era, calligraphy was considered a virtuous and pious act, and the katibs, and *khushnawis* were all deeply revered by the kings, princes and noblemen. It was considered the pinnacle of divinity, and the artist was uplifted along with it. The artisan became the mastermind—inspiring like the Prophet, untouched and pure like a holy man. The royalty often learnt the art from the finest ustads, patronizing them and offering high positions in their courts. Akbar established an independent department called the Aina-i-Taswir Khana, specially meant for training men to compile texts and translations,

and he had about 100 calligraphers under his patronage.[6]
Then there was the Shikasta style, mastered by Hindu
royals like Raja Todar Mal and Rai Manohar Das.[7]

'One's handwriting is like one's body shape,' Wasim
says as he puts away the books carefully, folding each
of them in a plastic bag. 'You can't choose how you are
born—fat, thin, round—but you can exercise to shape your
body. An artful hand validates good upbringing and good
lifestyle. Of course, your pen matters too,' he says, tugging
at the notebook a student places before him, chiding him
for using a split *qalam*. The chastened student hastily pulls
out another one, a reed with a tip like a pen. Sharpening
the pen with a penknife called the *qalamtrash*, he tests the
reed on the paper; a narrow groove is dented, into which
the viscous black ink used in fountain pens, known as the
davat, flows and remains contained, satisfied to have found
its right place on the paper.

'The best-quality qalams come from Iraq, but they
can be expensive. So we use the ones that are made from
trees that grow on the banks of the Ganga and Jamuna,' he
explains. 'Sarkanda, I think, is what they call the tree. They
also use sketch-pens these days. Useless things, those are.
No guile at all. But the computer-habituated hands these
days move flabbily over the paper with a qalam, rambling
on them as if lacking a spine.' He sighs. 'Look at this
poster; like most others, it's written with a qalam and the
Nasta'līq is specific to the rules that have to be followed by
this script,' says Wasim, pointing to a hand-drawn poster
on the wall—'*Insaan ki izzat hai jab woh kisi ka mohtaj na*

rahe [A man's dignity is maintained if he isn't dependent on anyone],' he reads out, his chanting tone tinctured with ominousness.

The annexation by the British and the toppling of the Mughal court was a watershed moment for the community of Urdu calligraphers. While the end of Bahadur Shah Zafar's rule was desirous for many, it was undeniably upsetting for others—especially for the region's Muslim population—and caused a severe blow to the Urdu language and the devotional arts. The introduction of lithography in India soon after was the coup de grâce. Katibs went out of business, but were mostly hired back by printing presses and Urdu newspapers, largely because printing technology[8] could not be a substitute for the fluid script, which was impossible to translate into movable type. And the last talents of the Urdu calligraphy industry in India continued to work for a while longer, writing out, by hand, any copy to be printed in facsimile. Urdu books were printed at Fort William College, Calcutta, in the Naskh style, which was similar to Farsi. Soon, the book market and the reading public boomed. Calligraphy not only reached a larger audience but also became more affordable. The slips of finger and nerves, and all those ordinary human uncertainties, no longer caused a furrow of worry on their brows. But, soon after, a company in Delhi introduced the Urdu Font Nasta'līq for computers. Not only did this take the specific personal performance out of the art, but it finally and completely robbed the calligraphers of their ancient livelihood.

'*Zindagi kya hai anasir mein zahur-e tarteeb. Maut kya hai ini ajza ka pareshan hona* [What is life but a manifestation of orderliness and method in elements. What is death but chaos within these same elements],' recites Wasim, the lines by Chakbast,[9] machine-printed in Nasta'līq on thick glossy paper, ready to be framed. Taking his thin spectacles off his face with one hand, he rubs the tiredness from his eyes, like a man who has been thrust into the sunlight after hours in cool darkness with such swiftness that he can barely make out the new images, aware merely of the speed with which he was thrown outside.

'The words are still around,' he murmurs, looking at his students, his eyes momentarily revealing a tenderness, an unexplained fondness for them—that perhaps confuses him as well. 'They are waiting to be released from the tips of the qalams.' The students stare at him, swallowing his words like water. 'Khushkhati . . .' he continues, mouthing each powerful word slowly, so that the power changes hands, from his memory to theirs. 'Khushkhati is so magnificent an art that it can be the greatest revealing power of a person. The words, the way the reed is handled, the writing style—they all can reveal a person's character, moral and cultural integrity, the entire psyche of a person. Each letter, each word, is practised so often that the soul of the art enters one's fingers. You have to control the concentration of ink, the compatibility of each letter, side by side. If they are to come from a katib's hands, the letters should carry a message beyond their meaning . . .'

Waving his hand dismissively, as if shaking out of a trance, he mutters, 'But this one is from a machine—empty. Anyone with a computer can be.' Fine print above a barcode in English catches my eye—'Made in China'. A nation, I faintly remember, whose governing party is officially atheist. 'So, art then has to disappear.' He smiles, but it does not reach his eyes. 'Unless, someone rubs the magic lamp.'

The class wraps up around late afternoon and the students quietly file out. Wasim stretches his limbs and walks out to the porch, looking at his students exiting the gate, back into the filth, murk and dust, the ordinariness of the megacity. 'In Japan, calligraphy is not just an ornate style of writing, but an event in itself,' he says. He speaks of the Kakizome festival, when they write their New Year resolutions[10] with fresh ink in their best calligraphy, which they have been practising for the past year. A few days after writing, they burn the paper on which the resolutions are written. The Japanese believe that if a tall fire is created by the burning paper then their writing is going to improve. Wasim turns to smile at me. 'Such is the regard the entire nation has for calligraphy. It is an art form that must be contemplated . . . not just read.'

8

THE BOAT MAKERS
OF BALAGARH

Come monsoon, the colour green parachutes down to this lazy hamlet of Balagarh in the Hooghly district of West Bengal. Creepers snake up tree trunks, draping the roofs and windowsills, wrapping themselves up telephone poles and latching on to wires. Frogs play hopscotch around puddles where worms make their homes in the rains. A drenched dog whimpers on its way, scavenging for leftovers. An oily slick of mud, resembling dirty cotton balls that have been torn to shreds, runs into an isolated home from which a sari-clad woman scurries out, looking up at the dark skies. She feeds fresh grass to her two goats and then places a clay pot beneath the eaves of the roof to catch the spill.

From a distance, a cacophony of axes and knives chopping through wood is carried by the wind and melts into this irrepressibly elating lilt of the rain as it dribbles on to the pots and pans through thick clusters of bamboo groves. Around the monsoons, every canopy lining either side of this pathway in Balagarh turns into a boat-making factory and the 400-year-old village of boat makers echoes with the sounds of their creation.

Legend has it that there was once a big, long river that gurgled down the Himalayan slopes and into these green valleys, over which thick willows of coconut trees bent, and a hot, yellow sun sank at dusk, giving way to thousands of stars that played by the night. Through the years, as the river traced its path to the Bay of Bengal, drying up in some places, creating new rivulets in others, it branched out like the thick roots of a banyan tree, intersecting the valley to create canals that flowed through cities and towns and, by the sixteenth century, into this little hamlet.

Almost a century after Vasco da Gama landed in India, European powers such as the Portuguese, the Dutch and the French followed suit, using the riverine route to reach further inland. Bengal's wooden boats often appear in the texts of this era, linking together pieces of history. In Abul Fazl's *Ain-i-Akbari*, they are mentioned as 'fine Bengali war boats', employed by Isa Khan in his fight against the Mughal naval forces under Akbar's illustrious general, Raja Man Singh and, in another instance, as 'a flotilla of 300 boats' used for naval warfare by Shaista Khan, the Governor of Bengal,[1] bought from local *majhi*s, or fishermen, in 1666 and used to defeat the formidable Portuguese pirates.

By this time, the Hooghly already had boats bobbing on it—boats that carried fathers, mothers, soldiers, dogs, cats, pots, pans, spices and fruits,[2] boats that arrived from Dhaka and Calcutta and the Hague and Rio. And Balagarh, a small village on the Hooghly, beyond its reeds and weeds, turned into a busy boat-making centre, carving boats of all shapes and sizes and, sometimes, ocean liners too.

A lean, wiry man sits with his lungi tucked between his legs in one of the empty sheds, smoking tobacco and taking shelter from the soft drizzle. 'When I was a little boy, my mother called me to take a puff. I took a puff. Then I loped down to the river and drank water from it, drinking so feverishly that most of it poured on to my shirt. Why would she or, for that matter, any person, put into their mouth something so nasty?' he inquires in a candid, boisterous manner, his voice gruff from all the smoke clouding his lungs. When he was sixteen, his neighbour, a fisherman who bought cigarettes from Calcutta's sailors, introduced him to smoking again and, since then, rolling beedis has become a necessary practice of thrift. 'I simply understand wood better when I smoke. It listens to me, moving with my hands and eyes.' Mohak Chandok has been practising boat making for a living in this yard for the past forty years as a seasonal rigger. The rest of the time, he takes his father's boat to fish in the waters around the coastal town of Digha, five hours away by boat.

'I grew up around the water,' he murmurs, taking long puffs of his beedi. 'In the evenings, we'd walk down to the river and I'd help my mother fish in the warm spots near the bank—throwing in cooked rice which the fish would gather around like bees to a hive. We would then quickly jab them with a spear and drop them into a bucket.' By the time he was ten he had started accompanying his father to the river on his motorless flat-bottomed boat that he had himself made. They'd be out for hours and he'd happily watch the oars hit the golden ripples in the afternoon waters—even though he'd miss a meal or two.

'Baba taught me how to build boats,' he says. He learnt the craft soon after he dropped out of school when his mother lost her life in a drunken brawl with his father. Mohak's father was a Rajbanshi.[3] With their place in the lower strata of the Hindu caste system, Rajbanshis are a fisherfolk community that claim to have been building boats for at least six generations.

Squashing the beedi against the rock that he sits on, Mohak lights another with a match. Taking a long drag, he continues, 'When my father wasn't passed out on the cheap *chullu*,[4] he'd tell me, "Feel the wood beneath your fingers, every time you start working on it. Learn to hone the chisel first and feel its vibration against the wood— all kinds of wood: babla, segun, sirish, khirish, arjun. Some woods might need a sharper blow." And when I would forget to sharpen my chisel, he'd smack me below my ear'—*thaad*—'like this,' he says, slapping himself on the cheek and then laughing as he rubs the sting away. '"Understand the quality of the wood," he'd say. "See the sal or the cheaper babla, and then understand the blade. Lastly, know how to govern your strength against the wood." Once, I cut my finger,' Mohak says, showing a scar on his finger. '"Put your finger in your mouth and suck the blood if you cut yourself," he'd say. Then looking at the gash, caressing it, he'd add, "Good, next time you'll do a better job on the wood."'

The rain stops and, for a while, only the roof of the shed drizzles water as it trickles down the slanted sheets—creating thin rivulets that make their way to the river. Mohak flicks his beedi on to the floor just before it touches his finger. The orange ashes scatter around the butt, turning grey. He watches it for a while and then takes off his slipper. For boatmen and oarsmen like Mohak, the boat is like their mother—the mother who steers herself away in danger, protecting the sailors in her sheltering womb—and one must not insult her with filthy slippers.

He stands up to join another worker engaged on the carcass of a boat, perched on stilts to the rear of the yard. They grunt to each other in acknowledgement and work without talking, each pounding on an end of this 15-feet long boat skeleton, the sound of their hammering echoing through the village, alternating with the threatening, thunderous sky.

For hours, they create the hull of the boat, pulling logs of wood towards themselves, hunching over them, measuring them to trim the plank and then heating them according to the arch of the boat. The woodchips have been burning for a few hours below the planks so that the rising smoke softens the timber. These planks will soon be joined by both the men and the cotton thread will be beaten into the gaps. A composite of cow dung and tar will then be pasted over these joints of the boat's body.

Mohak and his helper are the only two *mistri*s, or carpenters, in this workshop, while most others have five to ten workers at least. Together, they usually finish a boat in three months' time. After the boat is complete, they leave it to dry in the sun for a few days. Next, employing the ancient pulley-wheel apparatus, they noisily move the boat on a cot of oily logs to the river—amidst angry outbursts and curses in Bengali—and submerge it in the shallow waters to make the wood sturdier and, according to Rajbanshi tradition, baptize and ceremonially consecrate it as a 'boat', before giving it away to the boat owner the way a daughter is given away in marriage.

A Rajbanshi pandit is summoned for this ceremony. No women are allowed during the sanctimonious boat-building process, although they may help in cleaning the boat. The pandit bathes the boat with holy Ganga water, brushes its teeth with mango leaves, and several items that are gifted to a bride during her wedding ceremony are then placed on the boat—sindoor, conch-shell bangles, *alta*, a red sari—marking the beginning of a new life for the vessel, just as they signify a new life for a married woman. And then, in about two weeks, the boat is ready to set sail, away from the nerve-racking din, to find its own horizons and be caressed by the gurgling waves of the rivers, the music of eternity . . .

The boat-making business in Balagarh, though, isn't as old as the one in Tamralipta in Odisha, which couldn't withstand the fury of the seas, the higher production levels of seafarers from Arabia and China as well as the constant invasion by pirates. Balagarh, meanwhile, from various accounts in history, seems to be the natural descendant of Saptagram, near Bandel, a little further north from Balagarh. During Mughal rule, Saptagram became the centre of the local governors for sea-trade activities, giving rise to the development of the boat-making industry.[5] But in the sixteenth century, the main waters of the Bhagirathi river, which earlier used to course through Saptagram, started flowing through the Hooghly channel. The river flowing through Saptagram silted, gradually making it inaccessible to boats. The boat-making units, with skilled craftsmen trained by international crews who came with the traders, moved to Balagarh, abandoning the old town.

Around 1707, Raghunandan Mitra Mustafi, of Ula Birnagar in Nadia, migrated to Balagarh. The Europeans had made inroads in the incredibly navigable canal system, encouraging the boat makers, but Mitra finessed the craft by establishing an indigenous boat-building industry. He would carve out large, fat-bellied boats for the traders which would earn him a fortune while also encouraging migrants to swerve into this little hamlet, which soon turned into an industrial town where skilled craftsmen—both Hindus and Muslims—worked together in the hot, humid mulch. Mitra developed the wetland, building temples, a fort complex and homes. Soon, villagers dropped farming and took to carpentry, making Balagarh's boats the gold standard in India's boat-making industry. A moss-covered wall at the edge of the village that vanishes under the mounds is indicative of what was once a great fort, but temples with golden-yellow stones still dot the horizon, a robe of shining jewels in the green valley of ruins, just as old as the boat-making workshops.

Models of all kinds of boats, even steamboats with little glass windows, are lined up on a shelf in Mohak's shed. 'We make all these boats—whichever one you like—by hand,' he says. Mohak and most other boatmen can make a variety of boats—*patia*, a clinker[6] style, which has a small room where you can sleep and cook, can be traced back to the eleventh century with little variation as well as Balgarhi dinghies, *bali tolar nouko*, a slightly wider stapled boat.

Mohak builds the boats 'with [his] hands', a few tools and the river which, he says, is the 'ultimate authority' of his work. Quite assertively, it tells him if each plank of wood actually adds to the whole, and whether his craftsmanship is up to par. 'If the boat floats for a day or two without sinking and endures both nature and time, you know then that you've mastered this craft.'

Soon after his father's death, a decade and a half ago, Mohak awoke from a nervous dream, determined to build a boat in which he could sail up to the metro city of Kolkata and drift below the majestic Howrah bridge, where boatmen sing the soft, elevated notes of Bhatiyali[7] songs—the same ones his mother sang while smoking, Gopini kirtan or Kamla Ranir *gaan*, as they fished in the meandering river. Using his lifetime's earnings to buy expensive wood from Assam, he started working on the logs. He used the soft sal for planking, the cheaper babla wood for the decks, and bamboo, locally known as *gudda*, for the mast. 'There are boat owners,' he says, 'who look for aluminium seats and a steering wheel.' But he shunned them and anything else on the boat that was unrequired. He was not interested in self-glorification. He only needed something with stability in the shallow waters of the Hooghly—yielding to both breeze and billows. So he worked on it on the days that he had off from work. The dinghy took a year's time. 'Perfection,' he insists, 'takes time.'

On a warm, sunny April morning in 2000, Mohak set sail in his new wooden boat. The Hooghly had an opalescent dark hue that day, and in the shallower parts, it became transparent. It had a fresh odour, though, according to him. 'You could drink from it—just like that,' he smiles, cupping his hands together in demonstration. He flew past wild reeds and weeds, past narrow boats with sole fishermen catching a nap with fish hooks plunged in the water. He manoeuvred the dinghy through the zigzag path of the Hooghly, stopping every now and then for the *chira* his wife had packed for him. On the same afternoon, while he took a nap under a tarpaulin sheet erected to shield himself from the hot sun, dark clouds gathered above him in a hurry and suddenly the weather changed. A storm turned the river choppy, and his dinghy, not designed to handle any great amount of wind, got stuck in a whirlpool. Within minutes, it was swamped near a whirlpool and capsized.

'I drifted ashore, where a few fishermen from a nearby village helped me out. They later told me that all the parts of the boat floated away, except its mast,' Mohak murmurs, heaving before every word as he hammers the ply, working with it a little more forcefully than necessary. 'I still have the mast flying above my hut.' He pauses, looking up. 'I also heard that another boatman saw my sinking ship and was warned of the whirlpool. Well, at least one boat was saved that afternoon.'

In September of the same year, it had rained non-stop for a week, and the Hooghly, which spools like a paisley through the wetlands, started swelling. Within days, a massive flood smashed scores of small boats, knocked tree limbs through the roofs of several homes and inundated the huts along the river. The Balagarh boats turned into Noah's ark for the villagers. The boat makers saved the villagers, going against the current on the boats that were ready for delivery, rescuing them from water-logged areas and passing on supplies provided by the government. Mohak, too, joined them on his father's old boat.

Yet, to many of the hamlet's 500-odd boat makers, a big flood is just a part of the life one lives near the water. 'In the waters, even the most brain-dead nincompoop gets the fact that you're not protected any more. The weather conditions and the water are in total charge and you have to work with them to survive. But on land, man forgets he has to work with nature.' According to the transcendent laws that govern Mohak's Rajbanshi community, water—rivers, ponds, the water that is filled every morning in mud pots—is personified and worshipped. Rivers are compared to snakes—the female cult known as Manasa—that can turn vicious at any given moment

'In this world, each person and object, from the wood panels in this workshop to the trees here, is meant to play its part. And if you listen carefully, you can hear these things talk—the bamboo around here will tell you the message that the whispering breeze has left for you,' he says, his hammer drawn mid-air. Moving through his experiences, as if driven by some external force, the boat builder believes that each being in nature is given some role to play, and that when it is done playing its part in this world, it must die. 'This tree had to die to give way to a boat. My boat died to give way to another boatman. All the boatmen here will die some day, to give birth to new life by this river.' At least that's how the Rajbanshi pandit, the one at the temple by the river, explained it to him. 'Just as his role is to guide men to the home of God in the dark, he believes that my role is to make boats, here, in Balagarh and smoke beedis. Not to live in Kolkata and buy fancy cigarettes. The days I don't earn enough from boat making here, I fish. My wife hates it because I disappear for days on the river.' He smiles. 'It is peaceful out there.'

Mohak's workshop is close to Nimai Badi—Balagarh's biggest workshop. A few hours later, as watery sunshine filters through the clouds, workers appear in the yard. But they sit indolently, under the verdant latticework, the bamboo trees casting swaying shadows on their faces.

'They are on strike,' says Mohak, lowering his voice, sitting on his hunches beside me an hour later. 'I am not sure, but I have heard all this is politically motivated. The owner has political affiliations, and the party that he does not support wants their business to suffer. The other party may have paid the *kathmistry* union under the table to go on strike. The villagers here hardly have any love for politicians who have neither constructed roads nor subsidized wood for us. But every few years, they buy boats from the twenty-odd workshops during the run-up to the elections.' He smiles weakly.

The boat he is working on is to be sold to a political party. River campaigning is popular in these regions. Around election season, politicians, along with their followers, board boats that they sail down the river, stopping from village to village, promoting their agenda. They promise new roads, direct bus services and trains to Kolkata, or free foreign liquor. Sometimes, chilli chicken is on offer too. Other times, parties buy boats to distribute them to 'needy' people and lure prospective electors. But, otherwise, the boats simply lie in low tide on the banks or creeks, or are stacked one on top of another in the swamps behind the workshops, creating a flotilla of unwanted boats, the marks on the wood that appear during the clamping resembling the scars that the degradation of the Hooghly has left behind.

Mohak reminisces about the time when, in his father's days, buyers came in hordes. 'My father bought sal wood, which is good for furniture and boats. They had many boats lined up at the *nao thua*, the riverside marina. Slender, high-speed wooden boats were lined along with larger passenger-carrying dinghies back in those days. Buyers would come from the nearby Burdwan district as well as from faraway places in Assam, Odisha and sometimes Malaysia too. They'd see small sample cut-outs, examine the quality of the wood and come back a few months later to buy the boat. But, like the changing winds on the water, profits fluctuated quickly even back then, according to Mohak. The buyers bargained depending on the rainfall.

Fuller rivers meant more fish, leading to more boat sales and a higher price quoted for them.

A decade ago, there were more than forty-five boat-making units in the area. Today, they are just half that number. As West Bengal has slowly developed, bridges and ramps have been constructed across rivers, changing the way people travel. A couple of years ago, the fisheries department gave loans to fishermen under a special scheme. Most fishermen used the loans to buy dinghies, which was a godsend for the boat makers.

But the jubilation was short-lived—the fishermen's business depends on the Ganga, and water levels in India's longest river have been reducing due to the accumulation of silt. '*Gangai maach hobe na.* [There are no fish in the Ganga.] These woodworkers now work in paper mills in other towns, or look for jobs in those modish boat factories in the coastal town, Digha. I work to keep the tradition of these wooden boats alive. But, *niropta hobe na ekhane.* [There is no security in this business.] We'll make the boats. We have many hands. But who will buy them? Nobody knows about our boats outside Bengal. Middlemen are a nuisance. And if we can't sell a boat in six to eight months, who will buy the termite-infested boat? I asked my sons to look for work elsewhere. One makes grilles in Burdwan and the other is looking for work in Jaipur.' He shakes his head. 'The chemicals in the water are too many, I hear. I know the fish must die some day. But not all of them. Not together. Something has to change. Either the food we eat or how we fish.'

As I sail on an engine-powered boat past the village back towards Kolkata that evening, our attention is pointed towards a half-made vessel. Its two columns are carved at the crown like a race boat, tipped up and sinking. They unite as we pass them and then move apart, as things and people do in the water. The sound of hammering in the workshops is soon drowned by the engine. Slowly, Balagarh and its picturesque bamboo-lined streets become mere specks on the horizon as we drift away, meandering through densely packed moorings of fully made boats, their sails unfurled to seize any stirring of the heavy monsoon air.

9

THE ITTAR WALLAHS
OF HYDERABAD

A thick and sweet smell suddenly drifts over a swelling mass of shoppers haggling over wares near the Charminar,[1] as if cans of roasted dark sugar syrup have been emptied on to the streets. Walking through the arches of the old city of Hyderabad, I spot the source of the aroma—a tiny shop tucked near the walls of the Char Kaman[2] leading to the Charminar, which stocks hundreds of bottles on wooden shelves, each reflecting the intense beams of the shimmery light. As I walk closer, I spot a tall, broad man with a frosty white beard, wearing a woven skullcap, settled on a wooden stool behind the stall. He moves his hands smoothly so that he hardly brushes the glass bottles—slender vials, pear-shaped glasses, cut-glass jars—all made to contain some sort of magic, their shapes resonating the enigmatic properties of the fluids within. The bottles have glass corks that the man unplugs with his hands, producing a clunking sound, his regal nose deforming for a moment before regaining composure. With the unplugging of each bottle, thick fragrances escape. They are essences, extracts and oils. The smell of jasmine, rose, henna, flowers, air, water, sea.

'*Tashreef laiye*. Here, try this one,' says Syed Abdul Gaffar, an *ittar* wallah, smiling, laughing easily, weaving chaste Dakhni Urdu[3] into the conversation through the afternoon. A faint air of magic lingers around him, as if he were a wise old wizard pulling tricks on his customers with the worldly wisdom he has gained over the years. 'That's *zatar. Pur-kaif khushboo hai yeh* [This fragrance is full of intoxication],' he says in a deep, resounding voice, using the glass cork to daub a dot of perfume on my hand. The bottles have grown warm in the sun, so when he rubs the ittar on to my wrist, it seems as if it has been heated for the trial. 'It's made by diligently culling thousands of crocus flowers for saffron strands.' The thick liquid encapsulates the golden goodness of the sunlight in which it glows and then seeps deep into the skin, morphing into the body and, in a short while, becoming a part of you.

The noise around the historical monument of Charminar is overwhelming—cars, autorickshaws, women in embellished burkas, make-shift shops selling henna, glass bangles, stalls slow roasting *haleem* in large pots, fakirs with clay pots moving about in green *jubba*s, men with kohl-rimmed eyes—all clamouring for space in this walled city. But here, in this tin-roofed shop, as the twinkling lights are reflected by the crystal jars—blues, pinks and greens—to quiver on the old man, it is strangely quiet. Even calm and peaceful.

'*Allah pak ki azmat se* I have had this shop in my family for four generations now,' says Syed, cleaning the bottles with a soft loincloth before placing them back in their niches. Before they bought this box-sized shop from a landlord, Syed's ancestors played their part in an unwritten history. They sold their wares from a wooden box that hung around their necks, walking the streets with many others—bear dancers, rope-walkers, mango sellers, carders who buffed the cotton in old quilts, pedicurists who cleaned the feet of royal women with rose water and painted them with *alta*. They moved about the lanes of the old city that were lined with the nouveau riche homes of the nobles and relatives of the nawabs. Hearing their shrill cry, 'Ittar wallah!' echoing in the streets, servants ushered them in and the women of the household bought their scented wares; a vial of *raat ki rani*, a flowery scent reminiscent of breathing the warm night air of the streets, or jasmine that would lure their husbands to their beds instead of those of the courtesans.

'My grandfather established this store,' Syed continues. 'It used to be a larger place, but the municipal corporation wanted to station a drinking-water unit for passers-by and moved us here, near the Char Kamaan. They say that the one who quenches the thirst of the thirsty, the Almighty . . .' he pauses, looking heavenwards, 'will quench his thirst from the pure sealed wine of heaven.

'A birdwatcher learns to observe, a chef learns to taste. I was trained to smell. But the training was never formal. *In zeest ki rahon ne hi sikha diya khushboo kya hai* [The paths of life taught me how to smell].' He smiles, speaking of his education of the scents, moving his fingers like a bard singing ghazals before an audience. 'The smells of your childhood, for example, the rose petals that my mother pressed on to her neck and wrists for their sweet scent, or my grandmother chewing paan leaves stuffed with fennel seeds and slaked lime; the smell of my aunt's home who imported praying mats from Dubai, like the duvet in iron boxes that have been closed all through the summer. The smells have been retained over the years and become a memory. I very quickly learnt to translate them into my bottles.'

Syed grew up in the peaceful neighbourhood of Gowlipura by the municipal corporation office. Sometime in the eighteenth century his ancestors made their home here where he still lives with his two sons and their grown-up children, with a perfumatory on the third floor of the ancestral house, which he runs like Prospero from *The Tempest*, a second-sighted man with mysterious alchemical capabilities.

In this small room, the walls are veined with cobwebs and yellowed pictures of holy phrases from the Koran. Under greasy windows, copper pots, called *deg*s, their shine long gone, are placed. Syed keeps a candle ready, in case there is a power cut from the energy-deprived stations of his Telangana state, ready to search in the ash-streaked murkiness for his precious ingredients.

But today, the room is well-lit from a sole tube-light. From a covered cauldron, Syed dabs a bit of pink-tinged perfume on with a cotton bud and breathes in its scent, cupping his hands so the smell reaches his nose. A bouquet! Something incredibly uncommon and luxurious. He demystifies the smell for me, tracing it backwards to what had been blended into it.

'It is the humble *gulab*. Made with desi flowers, the ones with heavy petals, called the damask rose. They have the best fragrance. Our flower seller drops off these rare pink ones with the stems when they are available. The roses from the old bushes have the most pleasurable fragrance. But the time between cutting the flowers and making the ittar is crucial because the petals lose their essence with every second,' he says, snapping his fingers. Good ittar, like fine wine, depends on the essence of the year's harvest.

'Petals, after plucking, are then brewed in water on a wood fire overnight.' He enacts the process with his bare hands animatedly, breathlessly moving about the low-roofed room. 'And when these petals are plucked and added to the broth, they do not die.' He smiles, rubbing his hands together elatedly. 'They live instead, forever, bottled in these jars.'

Tiny cut-glass vials are piled in a carton at the end of the room. Once the ittar is made, Syed's daughter, a young, unmarried woman helps her father bottle the potion—pouring in the contents through the thin neck with a dropper. Does she sell the bottles at the shop with him? To that, he shakes his head furiously, frowning in disapproval. Syed prefers that his hijab-covered daughter work indoors. 'Shops,' he states, 'should display only wares.'

'The next step is essential,' he continues unperturbed, pulling up pellets of wood that fire the cauldron to make the ittar, in what is called the deg (still) and *bhapka* (receiver) technique. 'We use only *bainth*, or cane wood, not teak wood. Teak can make the vapours noisome, giving the perfume a bitter, seared fragrance. The fire under these degs is then lit with a boiler,' he explains, talking about the thin pipe through which he blows to tame the fire. 'I prefer cooking in my old copper pots.' These purportedly belonged to his great-grandfather. 'They heat evenly and pass on a more rustic fragrance to the perfume. Steel is bad. Very bad. I don't know why we Indians are obsessed with this cheap metal. Of course, one could use mud pots as well. My grandmother used to make *salan*, a spicy gravy to go with biryani, in old mud pots over wood. What a *zaikedar* salan that was . . .'

Connected to this steaming cauldron is another pot to which all the vapour is directed. Here, the vapour, called the *rooh*, is collected, separating the water from the oil. Syed generally keeps his ittars simple, mostly using this natural distillation process with sandal oil as a base. If it works, he bottles and sells them. If not, he is back at the workshop, creating another new fragrance and another and then another. It took him eleven years of training under his father to perfect his formula for gulab, a lot less than the two decades that his father took to perfect a musk fragrance. Gulab, resultantly, has sillage worthy of aristocracy.

Fables and legends trace the origin of this gulab ittar to Empress Nur Jehan, wife of the Mughal emperor Jahangir. But according to his diary, it was Nur Jehan's mother, Asmat Begum, who discovered the ittar instead[4].

The diary states:

I have regret for the Jahangiri itr [named after him] that my father's [Akbar] nostrils were not gratified with such essences. This is a discovery which was made during my reign through the efforts of the mother of Nur Jehan Begum.

When she was making rose water, a scum formed on the dishes into which the hot rose-water was poured from the jugs . . . She collected the scum little by little. It is of such strength in perfume that if one drop is rubbed on the palm of the hand, it scents a whole assembly and it appears as if many such rosebuds had bloomed at once. There is no other scent of equal excellence to it. It restores hearts that have gone [broken], and brings back withered souls.

The Mughals fragranced their palaces, anointed their wives and themselves in ittar, and sometimes offered the bottled sweetness as gifts to their guests from far-off lands. The women in the Mughal harem were educated in the art of enticement through fragrances, using *motiar* (jasmine) when the men were tired, and khus when it was hot.

'With the grace of the Almighty, the descendants of the Nizam's family still come to me to buy ittar,' says Syed over the racket as we drive back to his shop in an open autorickshaw, crossing the Mecca Masjid near Charminar.

'They particularly like the *oud* fragrance. Like the kings and queens, oud is a majestic, expensive perfume made from rare agarwood. Maybe it's one of the most valuable perfumes I have made. Fakirs often experimented with woods to burn beacons and bonfires back in the days of yore,' he explains. 'Sometimes, they mistakenly used perfumed woods like agarwood while cooking. When these woods are burnt slowly with sugar, they produce a thick, concentrated smell.' He closes his eyes, as if inhaling the smell. For centuries, the original location of the *bukhur* preparation was Yemen's highest peak, Shibaam. Scholars, writers, students and historians also used it in those times; it created a pious atmosphere of learning and knowledge. Some ingenious minds began bottling it and it became a favourite with the Nizams.'

He continues, 'I often import the wood now . . .' He pauses as the jangle of the rickshaw's unsteady body echoes in our ears as it is driven over bumps, squeezing through microscopic spaces available on the roads. A swarm of men in woven skullcaps walk out after afternoon prayers at Mecca Masjid as the auto stops at a signal. Some have dabbed *shamama* on their wrists, a light and viscous fragrance, perhaps taking a drop and rubbing it between their palms to beef up the smell with the moist heat. The women would have added a drop of *firdaus* to their pail of water, washing their hair with it. They leave behind a trail of fragrance on the street as they walk by, mingling with the fragrance of lamb roasting in ghee at a biryani house.

'Some say the Mughals brought ittar to India, but then I debated this with my neighbour, this learned Kayasth[5]. He says Ayurveda introduced it centuries ago, as long ago as the sixth century. It's just that they call it aromatherapy nowadays.' He laughs as we get out of the vehicle a few metres away from his shop, his time-worn, bony legs taking a bit longer than mine to unfold.

Tracing its potted history, the earliest distillation of ittar is mentioned in the Ayurvedic text *Charaka Samhita*, multiple references advising daily usage for its aphrodisiac and psychological healing effects. Varahamihira, the fifth-century scholar, jots down the method to create the *bakula* scent by extracting the essence from seashells by the method of distillation. Later, the use of agarwood oil is advocated in the seventh century in *Harshacharita* for perfuming rooms and oneself.

We have walked halfway across to his shop when he stops by the mosque; a shop worker is sprinkling water on the unpaved ground to prevent dust from flying around. The smell of the water on the sand wafts in the air. Syed stares at the worker for a few moments before walking up to him, cupping his hands before his pipe for the water. He splashes the cool liquid on his face and then combs some into his hair and sprinkles some on his kurta. 'Khakhi ittar.' He recognizes the fragrance—the one with the ephemeral smell of wet earth after the first rains, of humid, rainy Indian monsoons. *'Allah! Lajwab khushboo hai woh* [Lord Almighty, it is a fragrance beyond compare.] This fragrance, like Allah's first rains on dry earth, has been captured in the bottle after maturing wet earth in cauldrons. Which other profession can bring you so close to God?' He smiles.

'Most of our kind set up their shops here because it is near Mecca Masjid,' he says as we continue walking, leaving the mosque behind. 'One should always smell good near places of worship,' he whispers, quietening near a group of beggars clothed in rags, who sit, hoping for alms from the devout. 'It is abominable, to attend the mosque for those who have bad breath like them, or smell bad with odour from the armpits. It is *mustahab* to ask them to go away from the mosque. Ittar wallahs sit here to help people smell better. Our ittar is alcohol-free, and using alcohol for Muslims is forbidden anyway. But ittar . . . ittar is *ru parwar*. While bowing before the Malik, ittar deepens your faiths.'

'What about those who can't afford the luxury of ittar,' I ask him.

With that cliquishness that marks the cultural gatekeepers of society, he remarks, *'Har aadmi Allah ko khush nahi rakh sakta, na hi Allah sabka rakhta hai* [Not every man can make God happy. Neither can God make every man happy].'

Syed also has quaint statistics on his ittar. For instance, women from the old city like pure garden bouquets, whereas ones from the other side of the Musi river,[6] with bigger bank accounts, like fancy odours with no boutonniere smells.

'But there is one fragrance,' he says, seating himself back in his alcove-like shop, turning his weary, hardened body with some effort to pick up an ivory Belgian glass bottle, 'that everyone loves. Men and women. Hindu and Muslim. I created it.' Half of the nearby store owners say he couldn't have prepared it himself; the rest of them say no one else but him could have.

About six years ago, Syed concocted a perfume, stimulated by his hajj and the fragrances he picked up on it. Made of basil leaves, considered *shubh*, or holy, amongst Hindus, and popular amongst Muslims because of its mention in the Koran, it would be a simple essential oil brewed to just the right roast. Syed rode on his son's bike through a large farm that grew basil varieties on the fringes of Hyderabad. They journeyed past wild bushes and herb gardens. They sniffed camphor tulsi, which was rather floppy for the concoction they had in mind. Syed also crushed some beneath his fingers and ate it. They tried lemon basil then, which was sweeter, with a light smell. Finding it a bit too sweet, they returned, disappointed, but on their way out they were greeted with the sight of the humble holy basil growing in the wild. It was warm, nostalgic and slightly spicy, perfect for condensing into small bottled jars—and Nagma, a complex ittar, rich and fresh, simultaneously, was ready to be sold.

As the sun goes down, Syed and his grandson get busier, using cotton buds to dab dots of oil on the customers' hands. The customers try one fragrance after another. Syed sells shamama to relieve headaches and then *kewra* to cool an upset stomach. Most of the time, his customers demand to smell a memory—the powdery one that my grandfather used, or the flowers on the bed on my wedding night. One speaks the language of evanescence, while the other attempts to translate it—'You probably need an amber. No? What about champa then?'

Four or six tries later, the customer chooses a blend that will be mixed into a tiny vial of scent. A family from Dubai, here to get their son married to a girl from the city, wants to buy a scent for her, a traditional set of ittars in silver *ittardan*s—jasmine, rose, henna, garaj and harusa, flowers for different seasons. The patriarch of the family holds the soaked cotton buds under his nose and breathes deeply, muttering a blur of praises that turn one's head cloudy, just as perfumes do after you've smelled too many.

'It is like cool breeze on water.'

'And this has the silkiness of a cashmere shawl.'

'Exotic like the Al-Buraq.'[7]

Next, a brisk man from a nearby shop comes in to pick up a bottle of musk made from a secretion of the musk deer's bottom. 'Musk! Ah, musk.' He sniffs directly from a large bottle. The thing that he would wear to his cousin's wedding—a crisp kurta and a dab below his wrist, to woo his cousin's *sali*s. 'No, not this one', he says as Syed hands him an ittardan with musk and informs him of the price. 'I want the synthetic imported one. This is too strong actually.' And Syed forces a smile for him, muttering so that only I can hear, '*Naak par rumaal rakh kar bagh mein ghumne walon mein se hain yeh janaab* [He is among those who walk in the garden with kerchiefs on their noses].'

A few years ago, fancy synthetic scents were marketed by a few sellers from Kanauj, Uttar Pradesh. Synthetic scents are inexpensive, easy to control, and the best shops in the vicinity of Charminar started stocking more as the demand grew for the cheap, lighter stuff. Following their successful sale, most ittar wallahs started importing these fragrances, and so the men were doused in cheap jasmine and rose, like the smell of jelly beans, sweet, sharp and chemical!

'We had to start stocking those as well,' says Syed, pulling out a boxed bottle with synthetic musk fragrance made by a Muscat-based company. 'They don't have a nose for the ittar, these young ones,' he says. 'These fancy bottles are just illusions of the real stuff.' Like a beautiful three-storeyed stone bungalow with gardens, but only drawn on paper.

In the past years, Syed and the family's wealth has been growing, but the pure ittars are brewed and made lesser than ever. 'Twenty years ago, we made fifteen cauldrons a year. Now, I just make two or three ittars in a year. The rest are all imported from Kuwait, Dubai and Saudi Arabia.' The ban on sandalwood in some states for the past two decades has reduced the supply of sandal oil, making ittar more expensive than ever, the customers choosing the cheaper alcohol-based perfumes instead.

'I have never made synthetic perfumes with my hand. It's bad *iqhlak* [immoral],' he says. '*Allah ki dua se* we earn enough. I have bought a three-storied house and donated it to a madrasa. We live in another two-storied house with the families of my sons. I met with a road accident while travelling by autorickshaw a few years ago.' He points to his injured calf. 'I was advised retirement by the doctors.'

He continues, 'But this is all I know. I can't sit at home with my granddaughters and do nothing but eat and sleep, can I?' He waves his hand dismissively. 'If not money, my ittar earns me respect. I know my sons will have to start selling only synthetic perfumes soon, but till the time I am around, I'll keep making and selling pure ittar.'

He smiles, attending to another customer and another and another . . . until his job—of making this world a little more fragrant—is accomplished.

10

THE BHISTI WALLAHS OF CALCUTTA

Clouds in different shades of grey clamour for space in Calcutta's December skies, mirroring the people they shelter. It has started raining heavily, drops pelting the windowpanes of my taxi as it approaches Bow Barracks, a locality in central Calcutta—now Kolkata— constructed for World War I soldiers that today houses a diversified population of Anglo-Indians, Buddhists, Chinese and Muslims. Men scurry about, hurriedly wrapping their wares in plastic sheets and running for cover. When I open my taxi door, the noise, blocked until now, bursts in like waters from a flooded river, the ferocious torrent sweeping up with it everything on these cobbled streets—a babel of voices, a racket of rickshaw pullers, din from the coffin-making factories located close by, the clamour of food vendors, thunderous clouds, witticisms from addas, men heaving beneath heavy sacks, horns, cackles, sighs . . . wave after wave of it.

Large drops of winter rain pelt the backs of butchers skinning chickens near a mosque. Amidst the bloodied feathers of the birds stands a clumsily hunched *bhisti* wallah, a traditional water-carrier from ancient times. He holds on to the last threads of his ancestral profession, a bag made of leather, *mashq*, in the shape of an upturned goat, that contains about 20 litres of water. The legs of the goat cadaver stretch across his body, dangling listlessly, ending at a blue lungi hanging around his waist, legs bare to the ground. He stands there breathing it all in, staring at the water, blood and feathers fast collecting around his feet.

'Every evening, I come here to offer water to the devotees after prayers,' he says as I unfurl an umbrella for us. 'My father used to say, "Nawazuddin, you will wing your way to paradise with this relief that you provide to thirsty men,"' he says, his bare shoulders shivering in the cold. As the mullah reads the evening azan over the loudspeaker, I can only ponder over the providence. 'Bhisti' is a derivative of the Persian word *behesht*, meaning 'paradise', of blue rivers and verdant gardens.

'But this is nothing,' he mumbles, slowly nodding his head. 'On the holy days of Jum'ah, my father served water in silver cups outside Jama Masjid in Delhi, where we lived back then. "Drinking water in a silver utensil purifies the intestines," he used to say. We were then served *zarda* and biryani by the pilgrims who would soon embark on their journey for holy Mecca. They make do with plain *batasha* these days. When I stood close to my father I realized how big his bones were. There was also a moustache that ran up to his ears,' he recollects, licking his finger before gingerly perking up his own sparse moustache. A *khandaani* bhisti, Nawaz is very proud of his father's ancestors who served the badshahs[1] in Delhi.

As Calcutta nostalgists will tell you—preferably over an anachronistically priced cup of coffee at the Indian Coffee

House—in the slower and strangely unpeopled Calcutta of the 1950s, light years away from the theatrical exploits of wily men, you could see the lamp lighter put out the street lights at the break of dawn while a bhisti wallah filled his bags at the banks of the river Ganga, spending the morning hours watering the streets to settle the dust. Occasionally, when roads started being laid, the bhisti wallahs were brought in to water the pathway and, again, when the roadrollers were used to flatten the surface.

History has often been a spectator to the bhistis, who were, in the past, adjuvant characters in the narratives of battles and epics, and are now cogs in the machinery of everyday lives. And during the Great Depression of the 1930s, the bhisti was also an altruist, according to Samuel Murray who states so in his book *Seven Legs across the Sea*.

Thirsty children could be seen running to the bhisti with empty cups in their hands. The bhisti would release his thumb at the mouth of the bag and placed it over the cup. The happy children would drink and walk away. A mother, with a *matka* in her hand, would call out to him and he would wait until she caught up him. Murray informs us that 'the Indian mother might leave with him a pie. Rain does not fall in India at certain seasons of the year for periods of five to nine months, and water is water during most of that time. Should the water-carrier pass an ox, a goat, a dog, or a horse—anything in need of water—he at once eases his thumb on the spout of the bag and relieves suffering. The bhisti, in short, practises what Red Cross societies aim to accomplish, and what churches profess to do.'[2]

Tracing them further back in history, the bhistis were a Muslim horde from Arabia who are known to have followed the paths of Mughal ingression into India. Formerly, they served the villages and towns without any charge. But, with time, due to their popularity in the Mughal period, the bhistis adopted this as their source of revenue. Also identified as Sheikh Abbasis, they gradually suffused through the subcontinent, keeping alive their austere traditions as Sunni Muslims wherever they went, assimilating folk beliefs every now and then. Every Mohammedan family that could afford a bhisti would keep one to refill pots of fresh water from wells, lakes and rivers. Others, meanwhile, bought mashqs of water from them when required.[3] Hindus had *pani* wallahs who provided a similar service, walking around with earthen pots.[4] They were mostly Brahmins—upper-caste figures who also prayed and cleansed their sins regularly in holy water so that the water could be accessed by Hindus of all castes.

It wasn't long before the bhistis broke up into a number of clans, or *biradari*s—a few being Abbasi, Faruqi, Turkee and Bahlim. In the northern regions they appeared during Akbar's regime as the Abbasis who were the water bearers for the Mughal armies.

When Nawazuddin recalls their history, as told to him by his father, he speaks with gratification. 'My great-grandfather served the troops in the late-eighteenth century. The bhistis would follow them into the battlefields. Every time a soldier was injured, he'd crouch beside him, make a skin-cup with one of his hands and wet his lips.' Covered wagons, cavalries, foot soldiers, messengers on agile horses, gunmen, bonneted sweethearts—all moved around with the troops through war zones and cantonments; and among them would be the bhisti wallahs. In the infantry, a few would move along with every company, as would the barber and the washerman. The bhisti wallahs would escort the troops on their march, filling water in the mashqs from rivulets, cool streams in the forests or village wells as they sang the water-drawing songs of their tribes.

Perhaps the most famous bhisti wallah in history is Nizam Saqqa. Lore has it that the second Mughal emperor Humayun, while he was still trying to amalgamate the annexations made by Babar, was apprehensive of the complex river system of the subcontinent as they caused the loss of lives and farmers' livelihoods. His reservations were not unsubstantiated. After being treacherously conquered by Sher Shah on the banks of the Ganges near Benares, he barely managed to save his life in the inundated Ganga, all thanks to a bhisti wallah who supported him on his buoyant water-skin. Humayun rewarded the bhisti by allowing him to become king for a day—glorifying the bhistis—and the name Nizam Saqqa lives on.

'With wars in the deserts, where oases were miles away, it was the bhisti, or his mashq, that the enemy tried to shoot first. How do I know this? My great-grandfather lost a leg from a gunshot wound as he crossed the line of fire to offer a dying British soldier his water,' says Nawazuddin, crabbily brushing his bag, as though spiders had crawled up and made cobwebs on it.

'Our ancestors went around serving water from the mashqs to grouchy British troops, who often flayed, ridiculed and belted them on the battlefield,' informs Nawazuddin, gazing restlessly at the rain that has now reduced to a mild drizzle. 'In fact, they'd wake up devotedly at the crack of dawn, holding out water for the troops as they brushed their teeth or washed their faces, even before they themselves had their day's first glass of water in the parched countryside. They'd train us into thinking that were the lowly class, or that they were meant to be like this. But none of us thinks of ourselves as low or incapable. We always knew this was *zakat*, help.' Over time, like the other Muslim artisan classes, the 'bhisti or mashakwalas' have been granted OBC (other backward class) status, given their sensitivity to endangerment. Their community identity, though, continues to remain strong in some places, with caste associations like the Maharashtra Bhisti Samaj acting as a tool of community welfare as well as a pressure group on behalf of the community to avail the benefits of the OBC status. 'I knew of something like this in Delhi. In Calcutta, where we moved, looking for better work, there are too few, too scattered, too burdened with arranging food for the next meal to bother with the sarkar . . .'

Shadows of memories, those of the first, stinging awareness of classism, taint Nawazuddin's recollection of his childhood years. He puts these scattered memories together, slowly, shivering again as a soft breeze sighs past us. He remembers his father bowing before the babus in Kolkata as they walked on the streets, the babu's son instructing him to carry his school bag in exchange for sugarcane juice, or being served cold leftovers for dinner by a family to whom his father sold water.

'"Come, help me clean the mashq," my father, the big guy, would say. I also helped Abba carry his mashq, which was made of camel hide. It was a beautiful water bag, quite durable, unlike the goatskin bags we carry now, and it kept water from the tube wells cold for at least six hours without imparting any odours,' he lets on, forgetting for a while the time and his surroundings. 'On the nights when we travelled too far in the city with the water bag, we'd sleep under a tree. I would count the bats hanging upside down above me, staring into my eyes, perhaps hoping I'd play with them. But I had work to do the next morning, so I'd ignore them. They'd pester me, making clicking noises to nudge me awake, but I would press my eyes shut tightly,' he recalls, staring at the rivulets of sand, blood and feathers trickling down the street, making rude, lapping sounds. 'And while Abba poured water for men after namaz during the Holy fasting month of Ramadan, I'd sit on the benches outside Jama Masjid in Delhi, gazing at its minarets. It was such a beautiful pair.' An old married couple, maybe; calm, unblinking, keeping a close watch over the devotees. And the bhisti returned their favour too.

'I would be there to help Abba during the days of *roza*, providing cupfuls of water before dawn while the drum beaters[5] served their roles as human alarms, walking around the homes, waking people up for their pre-dawn prayers and feast. We went to their homes after that, filling water and then pouring it in the pots the women would keep out. We'd knock on their doors once the job was done and they'd leave us a few coins and, sometimes, a handful of dates, to break our fast. But the world has been evolving, and so have we. When direct water lines were provided to homes, and municipal corporations started providing water tankers to neighbourhoods, we had to migrate to Calcutta for work. I hated it. Delhi was calm and peaceful. In Calcutta, I felt a constant vertigo, *chakkar*, chakkar . . . like I had been violently cut and pasted from Delhi to this city. There were people everywhere here. Too many people. The city didn't even sleep at night. Butchers, vegetable hawkers, masjid, mandir, all coexisted in the chaos. I had to pay the local goons *hafta* to work here. It was in Calcutta that I started imagining the "red rains".'

'Red rains?'

'I kept seeing red rain everywhere, even when the sky was clear,' he says, shaking his head.

'In some places, the bhisti wallahs have switched to plastic and metallic pots, but their water does not taste as good. In here,' he pats the bag, 'the water is cool even in the summers. Today, the cost of camel hide is expensive and it's barely available here in Calcutta. Camels are desert animals that naturally try to retain water and keep it fresh the longest. Our ancestors used only those bags. But we use the ones that are made from goatskin.' He hesitantly pours some water for me in my cupped hands. Most of it slips through my untrained fingers and the rest of it smells like earth, like musk . . . like skin that is clean out of a shower. '*Thanda hai* [It is cold],' I tell him, and earn an extra cupful.

'Where does he get these bags made?'

'We sew them on our own, mostly, sourcing the goatskin from the tanneries in China Town or Tangra.[6] Most tanneries have now been taken over by Bangladeshi Muslims who don't make leather as good as the Chinese used to in my father's time. Even the shops that made mashqs have shut down . . . There is one guy, though, who still makes them on order. He lives a few streets away.' We decide to walk there right away, through the grime and gunk.

A little rooting through a few almanacs will tell you that bhistis were once cogs in the Kolkata municipal corporation machinery, watering roads and supplying water to those living in the sticks. Enter modern plumbing and soon they had to shed their key position as the water supplier of their neighbourhoods. Carriages, and later trucks, bearing water and supplying on call further caused the disappearance of bhistis. But with feeble plumbing in many areas, water wasn't supplied to homes in Kolkata regularly. They were a familiar sight in the Park Circus areas as they filled up buckets and tubs in the bathrooms of crumbling buildings occupied by Anglo-Indians and Chinese.[7] 'Handpumps took their place,' laments Nawazuddin. Now that most of these houses have been replaced by modern apartment blocks, bhistis too are on their way out. Miles away, they operate in a few pockets in central Kolkata. Bow Barracks is one such area where bhistis are still seen with their goatskin bags.

Seated beside the patio of one of the houses closest to the street, we discover another bhisti wallah—Saif, a dark, old man, probably in his sixties, he is far from cheerful about being buttonholed.

'Yes, I'm a bhisti.'

'No, my family is not here—my wife and my children all left me many years ago.'

'Why, I'm sixty-two.'

And then, when I needle him to say something about his day's routine, he says, 'Your questions are funny and beyond my understanding. Why don't you go look for someone else.'

'He is always a bit grumpy,' whispers Nawazuddin, drawing back when Saif starts forming his sausage-like fingers into a fist. 'When he was still in his mother's womb, his father and mother were travelling by train to Pakistan, where his relatives had settled. But his mother had to be taken off the train before they crossed the border because she went into labour.' Saif loathes that fact. According to him, if he had been born in Pakistan, he'd be a richer bhisti. No one is sure how he reached this conclusion; perhaps there was a massive bhisti migration to Pakistan in the nineteenth century and they switched to being small prosperous business owners there. Perhaps his mother told him this story every time she gave him a gruel of salt and rice for supper, but, even now, he resents having been deprived of a good life.'

Nawazuddin continues, 'I feel sorry for him, so I let him work in my area.' Bhisti groups operate in established areas, with tacit agreements not to impinge upon each other's realms. The aggregate number of bhistis, cited at anywhere from fifteen to eighteen in Kolkata, is unascertained. They charge six to eight rupees to supply water to the lower floors of buildings and a little more for the higher floors. A large amount also has to be capitalized for a new mashq every year. 'I service almost twenty homes in the morning and evening, filling water at the handpumps, and all the shops lining this street . . .' Nawazuddin says, heaving as he drags his bag through the streets of old Kolkata—Tiretti Bazaar, Kalakaar Street and then Burra Bazaar—a mishmash of wires, glutted buildings with people packed like sardines together, their locked windows choking them within, the swollen doors of long-discarded homes creaking from the damp air. Peculiar insects appear like redundant thoughts around the sleeping handcart pullers, buzzing unsolicited conversations in their ears, flitting away just as quickly.

Under a craggy makeshift tent full of tools and bits and scraps of tanned animal skin, we find Rashid, a rotund man with a toothless smile, chatting with a group of indolent men, mostly chewing tobacco and playing with stone chips on a dirty mat.

'I have been very happy since I moved here from Bombay about thirty years ago. My relatives, mostly bhistis, and their families, used to live in this area—all of us bhistis usually live in a cluster,' says Rashid, pointing in the direction beyond the masjid. This was in the last century, when housing was pigeonholed according to the vocation of the people from various castes. 'But no one who lives in these houses is a bhisti any more. We make do with huts in the surrounding *para*s. I make bags now. And repair shoes and belts for a living.

'We make world-class mashqs,' he continues, waving his hand at the four mashqs tied on to a hook. 'In a good season, my father would have thirty mashqs hanging in our shop. Goatskins would come from Punjab, buffalo skins for the belt and buckle from Uttar Pradesh. We cured them in salt, then cooked them in Dalda, and polished them with the lids of tobacco boxes. It would take two months to make one. A lot of hard work . . . They are still in demand. I still sell at least five a month, all buffed with ghee,' he boasts, while Nawazuddin jeers at him with an extravagant sneer. 'Rashid bhai, look at your patched kameez before you lie.' Rashid ignores him after a hard stare, disappearing into the back of the shop, mumbling cuss words under his breath.

'He barely sells two or three a month,' Nawazuddin whispers through his teeth. 'And he doesn't make them with ghee. The mashqs aren't how they used to be.'

'Have you heard of traders from Iran and Iraq who could be interested in mass-manufacturing similar bags for travellers in the deserts? Maybe that could help your business survive?' I ask the gathering.

'Don't build castles in the air,' an elderly man in a skullcap, who has crept up to the edge of the crowd, suddenly roars. 'Everybody is cattle for breeding now.

Buffalo skin is expensive and I have heard they have banned it some states. Hindus anyway refuse to drink water from these mashqs . . . It is a *paap*, they say. Why waste time, madam? Talk to those mineral-water-bottle wallah companies. That is the future. This Nawaz fellow, he is blessed to be alive after all these years of dragging that mashq around.' He shakes his head.

'There are times when I go to bed and I feel I'll never wake up again,' whispers Nawaz, lifting his mashq back on his shoulders, goatskin patches sewn on in several places with thick thread. 'What is the point, anyway? We earn extra money only if someone sleeps beyond their everyday alarms, or forgets to switch on the municipal taps in their kitchen, or needs more water for visitors,' he says, walking back towards the masjid where he lives. 'There's no more money in this job,' he sums up, removing his now-creased thumb from the enclosed mouth of his leather bag to pour some water for a street dog. 'Sometimes, I do not even have the wherewithal to feed my three children. From where will I find the money to teach them after the government school closes?' he says. I look into his eyes at this point. They stare back at me, tired of everything. A terrible exhaustion.

'What about the OBC benefits?' I ask him.

'Who has the money to get the certificates made,' he snaps back. 'So many babus there! That can take a lot of money.'

Saif, Nawazuddin and most other bhistis are bent forward, and they lean to the left, which is accounted for by their carrying of the bag on that side. But the crushing blight is the toll this labour-intensive work takes on them: 'Remedies from our *para* people keep me going,' he adds. Bhistis mostly resort to *al-Tibb al-Nawabi*, or the medicine of the Prophet, a loosely defined discipline of traditional herbal remedies based on the Koran and other Islamic texts. 'It relieves the pain, but doesn't restore anything. The doctor says my knees and hipbone have all taken a beating from carrying water from corner to corner on the streets and up edifices for over twenty years now. Sometimes, my charitable neighbours step in. But there is only so much that they can do.'

Vertigo deeply affects Nawazuddin. Perhaps it is the fall on the head he took a few years ago, when climbing the stairs of a building to deliver water. 'The red has intensified in my eyes, and the rain seems to fall harder and harder. At times, my emotions are so raw, I can't even tell what is real and what are just my thoughts. My wife thinks I'm going mad. She quietly listens as I often rant. She sometimes takes the children out to buy sherbet when this happens. But I don't even bother—or simply don't have any power left—to figure out what this red rain is and why I see it, everywhere, all the time,' he says as turns on to the main roads again.

Why doesn't he look for other work, I ask him. 'Nobody will give work to a hag like me. Carrying water, keeping it cool, knowing which handpump in the area is rusted and which one has the least sullied water—that is all I know. At least I'm not someone else's servant with this job,' he says, shivering a bit as a breeze blows past. 'I'll marry my daughter off and slow down . . .'

'Does she go to school?' I ask.

'No, she never went. We don't send our girls to school. They must stay at home and learn to be good wives. My son, he has to look elsewhere. Become a driver maybe,' he says, guardedly, murmuring something about their salaries and air-conditioned cars. For Nawaz, there was a clear route tracing back to his ancestors that was tangible, but erasing this path for his son is inevitable. 'At least my grandchildren will have a better life.' While, he, a bhisti wallah will become a story for them.

It's getting darker. But for Nawazuddin, the day has not yet ended. There is water to be delivered from his almost-inexhaustible mashq to a family of eight. They have hired him, briefly, until the government fixes their water pipes. He walks away, pulling the mashq back on as it slips from his shoulder—struggling to carry the burden of the past that this profession has bestowed upon him.

11

THE LETTER WRITERS OF BOMBAY

Dilip Pandey sits behind a wooden bench flanked by plastic sheets—he is clad in dark pants and a white shirt, the lapel streaked with sweat marks; the bottoms are oddly short, revealing his mismatched socks. An ink spot stains his shirt pocket, a hallmark of his profession. He pats his oiled hair nervously and often, but his fingers are steady. Stretching his lips in a tight, rehearsed smile, he says, 'It is tragic that we letter writers are done with our time here.' A weary disinterest filters through his words, as if narrating the plot of a long, dull book.

Over the last few years, scribes from tabloids and journals have been dropping by his establishment every few weeks for a bankable story, which is something of a contradiction because it relates to Dilip's flip in fortune. 'They want to know how we feel about the death of letters, stamps and the post office. Mostly, I tell them it's sad. But all I want to tell them is to get the hell out of here,' he mutters, his voice dry and grating, seared by the polluted air of Bombay. Instead, he tells me, he finds himself nodding his head politely, conveying the expected sadness over their fast-decaying legacy.

Dilip is stationed under a tent along with a few other colleagues, opposite the heritage structure of the Mumbai

General Post Office—now shedding gargantuan flakes of plaster, its windows rattling in its frames every time a door opens in this British-era structure, the sound drowned out by the commotion caused by the hundreds of passing cars and the mass of humanity on the streets. A couple of decades ago, when the air outside this gigantic structure was still fragrant with the smell of champa trees and the cobbled streets held but a few rusty Premier Padminis, Dilip started working with about twenty of his colleagues outside this GPO. He would lend an ear to a largely illiterate India, penning letters on their behalf to be dropped into the red letter-box. The letters would then make their indefinite and, most likely, laborious journey by truck, train, ship, camel, donkey either to the next state or across many time zones to places that you and I can't even begin to envisage.

An ailing father and dwindling finances brought Dilip to Mumbai. 'I was fascinated with this city,' he says, easing into the conversation, reclining in the chair, crossing his legs at the ankles and intertwining his fingers over his stomach. 'Bombay tells you a new tale every day. It speaks, this city, of people who are stumbling as they learn to walk, or of those who have learnt to talk its talk. But nobody learns to breathe here.' He smiles, wistfully and wearily. 'If you stop for a breath, you will die of hunger. Gourishankar told me this the day I arrived here.'

After a two-day journey from Varanasi, Dilip spent his first few nights with a relative's friend, Gourishankar. He hailed from Dilip's home town—a large, burly man with a hirsute chest and a vast mouth that curved downwards; he had developed, by osmosis, the disposition and mannerisms of Bombay.

Gourishankar gave Dilip lessons on letter writing. He took him around the circuitous GPO and pointed out some influential people who got the post offices running; he made him admire the city's deep, dark underbelly; he narrated the great tales of how to handle clients depending on their backgrounds—brief with ex-criminals, tart with daily-wage workers and chatty with government office peons. He painted the canvas of letter writing in a few simple strokes: 'Listen, write two lines for one word and do not forget to write "Missing you" at the end of the letter. It makes the wives and lovers happy, and the senders, in turn, happier.'

'The railways, postal services . . . would be but shards of broken glass in this massive country, divided by great rivers and mountains, if it wasn't for the British. India owes the British a lot,' Dilip declares, launching into a long monologue on how good the colonizers were for the country, lightly rubbing the thicket on his forearm as he speaks, as if congratulating himself. After the British set up India's modern postal network in 1854, they introduced professional letter-writing services outside the post offices, allocating licences to the letter writers.[1]

'Gouri told me I could be popular as a letter writer because I knew a lot of languages. I could read and write in English, Hindi and Sanskrit already, and while I was in Bombay, I also quickly picked up Marathi from the newspapers and the locals,' he reminisces. 'I read cartoons in local newspapers, heard the Marathi channels on the radio every morning for an hour.'

Over the years, he established a work ritual that involved arriving early in the morning, feeding the pigeons swarming the square outside the GPO, offering a short prayer to the idol of Ganesha placed on his office desk and then, finally, taking in his first client at nine in the morning while sipping a thimbleful of tea from a chai wallah stationed outside. Life, for him, started emulating a recognizable, comfortable pattern until things started changing in 1995.

'Somehow, the city just became bigger and we became smaller,' he mumbles, his gaze dull and fixed in a faraway stare. Bright lights illuminated the sky, the stars were losing their shine and the fireflies were vanishing. Cars moved inch by inch on the roads outside and people were flipping each other off at every intersection. The post office was declared a heritage site and the entire letter-writing squad was relocated across the street.

Sunlight trickles in through a fissure in Dilip's tent this morning; dust particles floating in the rays briefly reflect off a tin box that lies below his table, emphasizing its existence—the lid is cracked at the edges and coated with rust. Following my eyes, Dilip puts the box on the table, cracking it open to reveal its contents—folded sheets of yellowed paper, envelopes and used nibs. He takes out an old letter, a single sheet with writing on both sides, devoid of lines, margins, texture or print.

'I had written this for a client, a love letter for his girlfriend in Sholapur, and penned some lines from

Hemant Kumar's songs, my favourite.' He sports a hesitant smile, his eyes trained on the letters in his hand.

Dilip sometimes saves drafts like these, of the letters he writes for his clients, particularly the love letters to their girlfriends. 'The ones to the wives were simpler, with directives like "Pay the rent", or "Take care of my mother." Like this one . . .' He places an unpretentious, soggy blue paper before me. It is double-sided like a book, the kind that was sold at post offices in those days. The handwriting, taut and wiry, has faded into blue marks over time. The letter F resembled an elegant old man, slightly bent at the shoulders; the Gs and Ys are rendered with a loopy end.

An idiomatic vitality—with large lettering and simple phrases—keeps the writing light and easy, a style worked upon to simplify it for his readers across the countryside. 'All kinds of people came in to have their letters written here.' He makes a sweeping movement with his hand, presenting his humble street-side office to my scrutiny: a battered briefcase and old calendars stacked against the walls, and newspapers in various languages. A cat cosies up on the wall that is used as support to build the tent, graffiti painted in red announcing: 'Do not pass urine here.'

An extraordinarily diverse cross-section of humanity lives in this city in pursuit of the glittering Bombay dream. The hectic metropolis in a flux of growth attracts all sorts of workers—traders, hawkers, cooks and labourers with little or no education migrate here from Bihar, Odisha and

Uttar Pradesh. Girls and boys flock here from towns and villages. Sometimes, they end up looking down at you from the movie and TV-show billboards, beautiful and unreal. But most of them end up where they never intended to be—in slums, on footpaths, in red-light areas.

Dark clouds gather over us as he speaks. Dilip looks leaner and murkier as the evening sets in. 'Lots of young girls from Grant Road came in back then.' He refers to Mumbai's largest red-light area, where women usually end up when they have no other way to eke out a living.

'One of them, Swati, was very intelligent. She had been told by a lady in her village that she could get beauty-parlour work in Bombay. Upon arrival, she learnt that she owed the lady more than 1500 rupees and that the parlour job did not exist. She called me *bhaiya* and said she was twenty-five, but actually looked thirty,' Dilip reminisces, glassy-eyed. 'She sent letters with money to her son who lived in a hostel. Sometimes, she lied to him about the money, saying she'd been promoted at the sari shop where she worked; at other times, she said it was a Diwali bonus,' he says.

'In the nineteenth century, there were too many illiterate men away from home, and letters and telegrams were the only forms of communication. Letters being the warmer cousin,' says Dilip of the art that constructs tiny bits of individual history as it unfolds. 'I had some regular customers back then, like this sardar who drove a truck, but didn't know how to count money. He sometimes came with gunny sacks full of notes, mostly one-rupee. We counted the money through the day and attached it with letters full of instructions from the city workers on how to spend the money; bags of their notes and coins would lie with us the entire day, but never did a rupee go missing. Such was the trust back then.' He sighs.

'Many customers would be up well before dawn and spend almost no waking hours at home. They were too tired to communicate and expected us to add some embellishments. This was not the time of WhatsApp and SMS. Without the help of facial expressions, gesticulation, we had to communicate effectively and personally, and send something to an unseen recipient . . .' He taps his fingers on the tin box, unconsciously creating music reminiscent of happier days; perhaps he is remembering the stories he wrote that he thought the recipients of the letters would want to hear, the lies he created that they would want to believe in, the words that would have impressed them.

A wonderful code in stamps, for secret lovers, is another of the many things that have died with the art of letter writing. By tilting the one-rupee Gandhi stamps at strategic angles, messages would be communicated. Depending on the angle, the stamp could mean 'I love you' or 'Come and visit me.' This sightless correspondence of letters, and the vulnerability and valour that it inspired, brought out the confessional and, sometimes, the crazy.

'A lady came up to me once, in a burka. Speaking through her *naqab*, she said she wanted me to write a letter for divorce.' He smiles, opening his Pandora's box of memories. 'I could make out that she was crying and pretended to be busy with other customers. She waited for a while and then sauntered away. The next day, she returned, and I was thinking of more excuses when she said it was a misunderstanding with her husband that was resolved thanks to his sister and that the divorce was off the table. I couldn't have been more relieved,' he says, patting his hair again. 'Court cases can be messy.'

Dilip also provided reading services. 'My clients trusted me with their messages. There were messages for ex-criminals and traders, messages from lovers involved in extramarital affairs and messages from childhood friends,' he mutters, as if delving into the corners of his memories that have lain untouched for a long time. The business was not exempt from error as there were delayed news of deaths and births that occurred months ago, misspelt words in letters that flew across the states smelling of cigarettes, car grease or sambar masala.

On some Sunday afternoons, Dilip took bus no. 49 to an old Parsi widow's house. 'She lived with her part-time nurse, and was partially blind, owing to old age. I'd read the letters she received from her son who had made his home in Trinidad and from a sister who was at an old-age home in Pune.

'We'd reply to those letters sometimes. She narrated and I wrote, informing them of the weather, of the kindness of her neighbours, of her knees growing stronger and how she could now make tea without any help.'

Her home, he tells me, was filled with old china and tablecloths she had knitted when she had better eyesight.

She subscribed to a newspaper even though she couldn't read. Her apartment reeked of hospital sheets, garlic and Tiger balm—a smell that floated up Dilip's nose until it reached a corner in his head where he had preserved the memories of his long-gone family. 'I charged her half the usual price. She was particular about my handwriting though. Always insisted on Calicut fountain pens[2] with black ink . . .'

Thin sheets of rain start pouring down suddenly and the neighbourhood is plunged into chaos—men running for cover and screaming for people to give them way; a fallen button, a lost slipper, loose paper, worm-eaten leaves, all gather in tiny rivulets that flow down the streets. 'I doubt we will have more customers today,' he says pensively, looking out at the arrival of the Bombay monsoon.

For the letter writers of Bombay, things took a complete turnaround in this season in 2002. In the already-thriving mobile-communications market, incoming calls became free and Reliance announced its launch. Things quickly changed after that. 'I miss u' could now be sent via SMS in a matter of seconds to the deepest corners of bucolic India and directives to wives and mother were only a phone call away.

Priced at a few-hundred rupees, mobiles were in the hands of traders, hawkers, cooks, labourers and, over a few months, the letter writers were pushed out of business. In a matter of years, India Post stamped down on their business and postmarked it 'obsolete' in 2010.[3] The government's postal service decided not to renew the authorizations that allowed these letter writers to set up shop in their office quarters. And overnight, the letters writers' fate was decided—an obscure place in the memory of hundreds of those who went to them to maintain their links to their homes, families and friends.

A small man, dressed in a spotless white uniform, leapfrogs over the puddles towards Dilip, trying to keep his umbrella steady, but getting soaked nevertheless. Panting, he hands him a plastic bag with two books in it. *'Bhai,* urgent *hai. Ise parcel kar de meri* wife *ko,'* he pleads with the letter writer who mostly spends his time these days filling out forms, submitting money orders and wrapping parcels—the postal trivialities that have survived the extinction of his letter-writing trade. 'My son needs this book for his board exams,' the man continues. 'They live in Sholapur. Here is the address,' he instructs Dilip, who quickly takes the parcel, wraps it in thick white cloth and prepares a note with the address.

'What is your mobile number?' he asks the man.

'I have two. Write down both,' the man replies, smiling and explaining that he received one from the owner of the house where he works as a cook.

The letter writer snorts and notes both down.

Turning to leave, the cook stops in his tracks and turns around. 'Can you write a good-luck letter to my son? I'll send it along with the parcel.'

Dilip looks up in surprise and, without any other expression, pulls open an obdurate drawer, its channels disintegrating due to neglect, and takes out a letter-writing pad and a fountain pen, filling it up with fresh ink. When the nib touches the paper, it flows hesitantly at first and then creates letters and words. He closes his eyes in concentration for a few seconds. He probably wants to think before writing down every sentence because the reality of not being able to delete sentences, or shift passages or idioms around, is a bit disturbing. Opening his eyes again, he scribbles a few lines in Hindi; a fingerprint appears at the bottom of the page, where he holds the paper with his free hand; and a dog-ear has developed on the edge, where it was placed in the drawer, the taut, wiry writing blots around the punctuations, and it is nothing like the neat, ordered lettering from a computer.

But there is neither impatience nor bemusement visible in Dilip's writing. No problems of keyboard keys and printers for him. And here it is, in paper and ink, smelling of times gone by, a legacy that can be handed down to the cook's son—perhaps the last generation of people who would be given a handwritten letter—who'd suck its contents into the pool of his memory and relish the letter from his father who wasn't around for most of his years growing up. He will stow it away with all his other memories, the good, the bitter and the ugly, keeping them sealed, locked under everything else, and finally let them rust, until, one day, it will make its way into the hands of the people to whom letters are nothing more than antiques that have disappeared the way of papyrus scrolls, parchments and cablegrams.

'Monsoons have always been a time for low trade.' Dilip sighs. The other letter writers, sitting a few metres away from us, start packing up as the downpour thickens. 'But I have stopped caring,' he says, shaking his head, patting his thick, oily hair again. 'I earned enough to educate my son—*dekho na kismat* [look at fate]—he wants to join the communications industry. For every new job created, some have to be destroyed. Who wants to sit in this mulch now? A rat was nibbling at my shoe the other day.' He nods his head.

'Honestly, I'm done with writing letters. I was a fastidious editor. I chopped pitilessly from my customers' notations on some occasions and weaved emotions into others—not that I would get caught. I have too many secrets within me and cannot hold any more. The thing is that nobody wants to sit here now.' He puts on a raincoat, ready to leave for the day. 'I'll do away with this,' he says, buckling the belt around his waist and fastening the button at his neck. He puts the tin box in his briefcase and locks the bench to a hook on the wall. 'And use my savings to become an LIC agent. Mobiles and banks *ka zamana hai, bhai.* Post office *aur hamara zamana khatam ho gaya* . . . [It is the time of mobile phones and banks. The time for post offices and letter writers has passed . . .]'

Clutching his suitcase, Dilip steps out into the rain. I stop him for a last question. Does this upset him, this dying art or—if he wishes to call it so—craft?

'I don't know,' he says, lifting his shoulders in a shrug. 'It's all a part of the change. Like my son says, "It is the age of computers, learn it." And, as much as I want it to be otherwise, I can hardly tell him it's the age of handwritten letters.'

ACKNOWLEDGEMENTS

Writing this book has been a collaborative effort involving extraordinary people, but the biggest contribution is that of all the interviewees in this book, who let me in their lives, often, and let me be intrusive. These stories belong to them and I am but a mere narrator.

Through the course of writing these stories, I had to travel through the remote hinterlands of the country, conversing with my interviewees in many different languages. I am hugely indebted to many people for accompanying me, hosting me and helping me speak to them. Vinod Tiwari, Rakesh Kumar, T. Varaprasad, Satar Khan, Indrajeet Dasgupta, Abhay Bhadani, Ashok Bhati, Salim Ansari, my sister-in-law Prerna Kundalia, Thota Vinesh, and Fatik Khan and his grandmother, Kamerunissa Khan. A special mention must be made here to Laal Sahib of Ranchi for going out of his way to help me research one of the toughest stories in the book, that of the Godna artists. My biggest thanks would go to the selfless tribe of academics, professionals and authors who have given away their own knowledge and research for this book: Dr Saroj Rai, Dr Yash Patel, K. Mahender Reddy, Swarup Bhattacharya, Dr Vulli Dhanaraju, Rangan Dutta, Dr Hari Oraon and Muhammad Iqbal Bhutta. Also, a word for the librarians at the Asiatic Society Library, Kolkata, and the JNU Library, New Delhi, and their immense knowledge of archives.

Many were kind enough to read through my early drafts and/or offer their invaluable suggestions: Manu Chakraborty, Prateek Raja, Sriram Karri, Iftekhar Ehsan, Baradwaj Rangan, Sita Mamidipudi, Deepa Bhasthi, Damayanti Mukherjee, and my brothers, Devang and Soumil, who were always a call away. I would like to thank them and my mentors over the years—Namita Shrivastav, Pritha Kejriwal and Sayan Bhattacharya for widening my perspectives and building on my horizons. (Two of the eleven stories published in this book were first published in *Kindle Magazine*, in their earlier forms.)

My thanks to my editor, Gurveen Chaddha, for spotting my submission in a deluge of her emails and making this book happen. Her patience and care along with that of visionaries like Milee Ashwarya and Chiki Sarkar at Penguin Random House have taken this book far beyond what I thought it could be. A special mention to my copy editor, Rachita Raj; Vedanti Sikka, the cover designer of this exquisite cover; and the illustrator, Andrew Fairclough.

Through the journey of writing this book, the biggest lesson I have learnt is that humility is a mark of truly accomplished men and women. Both Shashi Tharoor and Gulzar Saab responded within hours of me approaching them for appraising my drafts and read through them patiently. My unbounded gratitude to them. Also, my heartfelt gratitude to K. Satchidanandan, Anees Salim and Kishwar Desai, for ratifying the stories in their nascent stages.

A huge thank you to my mother and father back in Hyderabad, for believing in my dreams much before I started dreaming them. My gratitude, also, to my other set of parents here in Calcutta, for their unflagging support and abiding faith in my decisions.

And lastly, to my rock and my favourite travel companion, my husband, Vivek. This book wouldn't have been possible without you.

NOTES

Chapter 1: The Godna Artists of Jharkhand

1. Rajat Kujur, in his article 'Red Terror over Jharkhand' describes the kangaroo courts: 'Denial of justice is the most important reason for the establishment of a parallel judiciary in Jharkhand. However, the primary difference between the Naxal kangaroo courts and the subordinate judiciary is the time and cost factor. While the common folk have no way of reaching the existing judicial system, the kangaroo courts reach the deprived sections of society. The Naxals are the sole arbiters of disputes related to *jal* (water), *joru* (wife) and *zameen* (land).' Rajat Kujur, 'Red Terror over Jharkhand', article number 1881, Institute of Peace and Conflict Studies, 3 November 2005; available online at http://www.ipcs.org/article/india/red-terror-over-jharkhand-1881.html.

2. Nomadic tribe found mostly in Bihar and Jharkhand.

3. Jean-Baptiste Tavernier was a French traveller and jewel merchant who wrote *Les Six Voyages, qu'il a fait en Turquie, en Perse, et aux Indes*, which was eventually published in

Paris in 1676, and contained personal experiences of his trip.

4. Clare Anderson, 'Godna: Inscribing Indian Convicts in the Nineteenth Century', in *Written on the Body: The Tattoo in European and American History*, ed. Jane Caplan (London: Reaktion Books, 2000).

5. Kurukh is a Dravidian language spoken by the nearly 2 million Oraon tribal peoples of Orissa and the surrounding areas of India in Bihar, Jharkhand, Madhya Pradesh, Chhattisgarh and West Bengal.

6. Heinz-Jürgen Pinnow, *Kharia-Texte (Prosa und Poesie)* (Wiesbaden: Otto Harrassowitz, 1965).

7. The Oraons are one of the largest tribes in South Asia and are classified in the Scheduled Tribes list of the Indian Constitution. They mainly depend on agriculture to earn their living. They are also known as Kurukh tribes and have adapted a few customs of the areas they have migrated to. These tribes are mainly found in the states of Jharkhand, Bihar, West Bengal and Orissa. *See* Abhik Ghosh, *History and Culture of the Oraon Tribe* (New Delhi: Mohit Publications, 2003).

8. To make a man of him, an Oraon boy, at the age of twelve or thereabouts, has seven or more scars made on his arm in the following manner: Seven or more rings of cow dung are placed on the arm to be operated upon, and the skin beneath each of these rings is burnt with a lighted wick. In a village where there is a dumkuria, or common dormitory, for all the bachelors of the village, these scars, called *sika* marks, are made by the older boys on the arms of the younger boys when the latter are admitted into membership of the dumkuria fraternity. *See* S.C. Roy, 'Birth and Childhood Ceremonies among the Oraons', *Journal of the Bihar and Orissa Research Society* (1915).

Chapter 2: The Rudaalis of Rajasthan

1. Legend has it that the beautiful goddess Saraswati sprung
    from the forehead of her father Brahma, the god of creation.
    It is said that as soon as Brahma looked at her beauty, he
    was filled with desire for her. Unhappy with the amorous
    attentions he bestowed upon her, Saraswati tried to dodge
    and hide. This is why the river Saraswati apparently flows
    underground. And the brief appearances she made above the
    ground were the moments, legends assert, when she stopped
    to rest from her tiring run. Scientists say new evidence could
    unearth the Saraswati today and research in this area is afoot.
    See Richard Mahapatra, 'Saraswati underground', *Down To
    Earth*, 15 November 2002; available online at http://www.
    downtoearth.org.in/coverage/saraswati-underground-15455.
2. Statistics obtained from the thakur of the area himself; an
    approximate figure.
3. Rawat Rajputs were related to Maharawal Sabal Singh
    Bhati of Jaisalmer and are direct descendants of Kunwar
    Bankidas. The rulers of Jaisalmer are descendants of Lord
    Hari Krishna, a Yadu Rajput of Somvansha (i.e., the lunar
    or Indu race.) Prayag (now known as Allahabad) was the
    cradle of the race after which Mathura remained as the
    seat of power for a long period. They were driven out of
    Mathura after their chief was defeated and killed; they
    eventually settled in Punjab and Kabul, where they changed
    their patronym to Bhati, after a brave chief. However, his
    descendants were defeated by invading tribals and they
    shifted their capital to the Thar Desert.
4. 'Daroga' means the offspring of a Rajput father and a non-
    Rajput (lower-caste) mother. *See* Lindsey Harlan, *The

Goddesses' Henchmen: Gender in Indian Hero Worship (New York: Oxford University Press, 2003).

5. Daories often doubled up as rudaalis. The emergence of the daori caste is often associated with Rajput rule. They were sometimes admitted into the zenana (the part of the household to which the women of the family were restricted) and served as domestic help. Other times, they were maintained outside the homes in separate accommodation. *See* K.S. Singh and B.K. Lavani, ed., *People of India: Rajasthan, Volume 1, Anthropological Survey of India* (New Delhi: Popular Prakashan, 1998).

6. In India, dowry is the payment in cash or in gifts (jewellery, electrical appliances, furniture, bedding, crockery, utensils and other household items) made to a bridegroom's family to help the newlywed bride set up her home. The dowry system is thought to put great financial burden on the bride's family. The payment of a dowry has been prohibited under the Dowry Prohibition Act of 1961 in Indian civil law. See Maya Unnithan-Kumar, *Identity, Gender, and Poverty: New Perspectives on Caste and Tribe in Rajasthan*, (New York: Berghahn Books, 1997).

7. The Mirasis are hereditary bards of lower caste who are said to have converted to Islam about eight centuries ago. They originally belonged to the Hindu Dhadi caste.

8. Lindsey Harlan, *Religion and Rajput Women: The Ethic of Protection in Contemporary Narratives* (Berkeley: University of California Press, 1992).

9. During the marriage ceremony, the groom applies a red-coloured powder, kumkum, to the parting in the bride's hair as a part of the Hindu marriage ceremony. Subsequent, kumkum is applied by the wife as part of

her dressing routine to signify her status as a married woman. Once widowed, a woman is not supposed to wear kumkum.

Chapter 3: The Genealogists of Haridwar

1. Sapta Puri are the seven holy pilgrimages or tirthas in India, namely: Ayodhya, Mathura, Haridwar, Varanasi, Kanchipuram, Ujjain and Dwarka. In Hinduism, 'tirtha' connotes religious places of spiritual importance. The root word in tirtha is *tri* (in the Sanskrit), which means 'to get rid of all sins', a step towards the attainment of Nirvana or salvation.

2. Hindu Brahmin priests or pandits are popularly known as Pandas in Haridwar; they essentially fulfil the roles of family priests, pilgrim guides and record keepers for families; the term is generally used as a suffix to the names and often used instead of last names. *See* John Renard, *The Handy Religion Answer Book* (Detroit: Visible Ink Press, 2002).

3. The Great Plague lasted from 1665–66 and killed an estimated 1,00,000 people—almost a quarter of London's population. There was no one whose duty it was to report a death to anyone in authority. Instead, each parish of the city appointed two or more 'searchers of the dead', whose duty it was to inspect a corpse and determine the cause of death. A searcher was entitled to charge a small fee from relatives for each death they reported and thus it was noted. But many of these parish clerks who kept the records themselves died and the rest of the records were destroyed in the Great London Fire. *See* James Leasor, *The Plague and the Fire* (London: George Allen & Unwin, 1962).

4. Hsiang-lin Lo, *The extent and preservation of genealogical records in China* (Utah: The Genealogical Society of Utah, 1969).

5. The Kathats or Merats are a Rajput community from the state of Rajasthan in India and the provinces of Punjab and Sindh in Pakistan.

6. The scriptures, in ancient times, were written on bhojpatra (a paper-thin bark of the Himalayan birch tree) which never lasted in a readable condition for more than 500 to 800 years, even with extreme care. Some of the bhojpatras might still be available with some Pandas and are preserved in public libraries.

7. Besides being folk singers, Manganiyars are also genealogists and orally remember family histories. They also make shubhraj, which was sometimes an eulogy and other times a testimonial of the family and its history, which they sang at public places and family gatherings.

8. A traditional greeting for followers of Goddess Ganga translating to 'Victory to Goddess Ganga'.

9. The term *gaddi* means 'mattress'. Back in time, one-man offices were a mattress and a desk in a marketplace. Although brick-and-mortar structures replaced them, they are often known as 'gaddi', which essentially imply 'the seat of the owner'.

10. The Genealogical Society of Utah (GSU) is dedicated to gathering, preserving and sharing genealogical information throughout the world. Established in 1894, the GSU is an incorporated, non-profit educational institution entirely funded by The Church of Jesus Christ of Latter-Day Saints. In the 1990s, the church expanded the Genealogical Society of Utah and it eventually became known as FamilySearch.

Chapter 4: The Kabootarbaaz of Old Delhi

1. Charles Darwin, *On the Origin of Species by Means of Natural Selection, or the Preservation of Favoured Races in the Struggle for Life* (London: Forgotten Books, 2015).

2. Scientists at the University of Pisa have discovered that the secret behind pigeons' ability to navigate perfectly over journeys of several hundred miles is by creating odour maps of their neighbourhoods and using these to orient them. This replaces the idea that they exploited subtle variations in the Earth's magnetic field to navigate. *See* Hans G. Wallraff, *Avian Navigation: Pigeon Homing as a Paradigm* (Germany: Springer-Verlag Berlin Heidelberg, 2005).

3. For further reading about ishqbazi, see the website of The Packard Humanities Institute (Persian Literature in Translation): http://persian.packhum.org/persian//.

4. Edward James Rapson, Wolseley Haig and Richard Bur, *The Cambridge History of India* 4 (New Delhi: S. Chand Publishing, 1963).

5. Abū'l-Faẓl ʿAllāmī, *The Ain i Akbari*, trans. H. Blochmann and H.S. Jarrett (Calcutta: Asiatic Society of Bengal, 1873).

6. S.J. Monserrate, *The Commentary of Father Monserrate on His Journey to the Court of Akbar*, trans. J.S. Hoyland (London: Humphrey Milford, Oxford University Press, 1922).

7. Chawri Bazaar was popular for its courtesans in the nineteenth century, frequented by nobility as well as the rich. With the British, *tawaif*s receded into the background and prostitutes came to occupy the upper floors of the market. This eventually led to the area becoming a hub of criminality and thus the Delhi Municipal Committee evicted them from the area, altogether, with most moving to the GB Road area.

8. Indian Wildlife (Protection) Act, 1972.

Chapter 5: The Storytellers of Andhra

1. Makar Sankranti is one of the most important festivals of the Hindu calendar and celebrates the sun's journey into the northern hemisphere, a period which is considered to be highly auspicious.

2. A Tanjore doll is a type of traditional Indian bobblehead made of terracotta material. The doll's head moves in a continuous dance-like motion because its centre of gravity and total weight is concentrated at its central core all the time.

3. The forerunner of the Burrakatha was known as the Jangamkatha, literally translating to 'the stories of the Jangam tribe'. The storyteller, accompanied by his wife, would travel from village to village, performing for two to three days at a stretch. This then became a popular form called Burrakatha which was used for political purposes and social messages, the performance often laced with sarcasm.

4. The Budaga Jangalu are listed in the Ninth Schedule of the Constitution as a scheduled caste community that has lived in history as alms seekers and hunters, reciting Jangamkathas for a living. *See* Nagendra K.R. Singh, ed., *Global Encyclopaedia of the South Indian Dalit's Ethnography*, vol. 1 (New Delhi: Global Vision Publishing House, New Delhi).

5. Virasaivism, or Lingayatism, traces its origin to the five great religious teachers, Renuka, Daruka, Ghantakarna, Dhenukarna and Visvakarna, who, according to tradition, were the earthly manifestations of the five aspects of Lord Shiva. The religion was later made popular by Basava, a preacher and saint and Revanasiddha. Virashaivnism was a reformist's movement on the lines of the Arya Samaj in

the nineteenth century. *See* Homer Alexander Jack, ed., *World Religions and World Peace* (Boston: Beacon Press, 1968).

6. On 2 June 2014, Telangana was formed as the twenty-ninth state of India, separating the former state of Andhra Pradesh into two.

7. The large black carpenter bee.

8. Country liquor.

9. The 'Fourth Wall' is a theatrical term for the imaginary 'wall' that exists between actors on stage and the audience. Obviously, no such wall really exists, but to keep up the illusion of theatre, the actors pretend that they cannot hear or see the audience and the audience gets to enjoy the wonderful sensation of being a fly on the wall.

10. The Telangana Movement refers to a people's movement for the creation of the new state of Telangana from the existing state of Andhra Pradesh in South India. The proposed new state corresponds to the Telugu-speaking portions of the erstwhile princely state of Hyderabad. The Union Cabinet, on 7 February 2014, unilaterally passed the bill for the creation of Telangana, clearing the way for its introduction in Parliament. This has been one of the most controversial movements in South India.

11. The Praja Natya Mandali emerged in 1943, having been inspired by the establishment of the Indian People's Theatre Association (IPTA) by progressive writers. In the initial years of the organization, the activities of the association were confined to the Krishna and Guntur districts. Gradually, however, the Mandali extended to other parts of Andhra Pradesh as well. Under the leadership of Garikapati Rajarao and Koduri Atchaiah, the Praja Natya Mandali conducted district workshops and taught youngsters the performatory

methods of Telugu folk forms including Burrakatha. As the leading radical cultural group of the time, it was almost inevitably drawn into the Telangana Movement and began to play an active role in it. *See* Ananda Lal, ed., *The Oxford Companion to Indian Theatre* (New Delhi: Oxford University Press, 2004).

Chapter 6: The Street Dentists of Baroda

1. A 'torus' is a harmless growth of bone in the mouth.
2. A. Coppa et al., 'Palaeontology: Early Neolithic Tradition of Dentistry', *Nature* 440 (7085) (6 April 2006).
3. Josephine M.T. Khu, ed., *Cultural Curiosity: Thirteen Stories about the Search for Chinese Roots* (Berkeley and Los Angeles, California: University of California Press, 2001).
4. Ahmad Ka Mohalla is a street in Chandni Chowk, Delhi, now known as Krishna Gali. It was known to be inhabited by the affluent, mostly Muslims. Many families that lived here were looted and destroyed during the days of the Partition, and the area was later occupied by Sikh families.
5. Madehow.com, 'How to Make Dentures', vol. 3; available online at http://www.madehow.com/Volume-3/Denture.html.
6. Smokeless tobacco.
7. Jo Johnson, 'India's Street Dentists facing decaying business', *Financial Times*, 3 November 2007; available online at http://www.ft.com/cms/s/0/51f29222-899f-11dc-8dff-0000779fd2ac.html#axzz3s0n3DWs7.
8. 'Gendarmes round up "Dodgy Dentists",' BBC News, 11 September, 2003; available online at http://news.bbc.co.uk/2/hi/europe/3100490.stm.

9. Khwaja Jamal, 'Bitter pill for fake dentists', *Telegraph*, 22 July 2011; available online at http://www.telegraphindia.com/1110723/jsp/bihar/story_14274077.jsp.

Chapter 7: The Urdu Scribes of Delhi

1. The imperial capital of Shahjahanabad was built by the Mughal Emperor Shahjahan (1628–58) between 1639–48, and it spread out over a large area along the banks of the river Yamuna in the south-eastern parts of the Delhi triangle. Today, what remains are the crumbling walls, gates and a few majestic buildings like the Red Fort and the Jama Masjid. *See* Stephen P. Blake, *Shahjahanabad: The Sovereign City in Mughal India (1639–1739)* (Cambridge: Cambridge University Press, 1991).

2. Manjusha Madhu, 'The Art of Devotion and a Devotion to Art', *Sunday Guardian*, 20 May 2012; available online at http://www.sunday-guardian.com/artbeat/the-art-of-devotion-a-a-devotion-to-art.

3. Diwani is an Arabic script first invented in the fifteenth century and later developed during the reign of the early Ottoman Turks (from the sixteenth to seventeenth centuries). It was used in the Ottoman courts, and the rules of this script were kept a secret, confined only to its masters and a few bright students; it was mostly used for official purposes.

4. The Nasta'liq script was a predominant style of Persian calligraphy during the fifteenth and sixteenth centuries. A cursive script, the Nasta'liq was a combination of the Naskhī and Ta'liq styles, featuring elongated horizontal strokes and exaggerated rounded forms. The diacritical marks

were casually placed, and the lines were flowing rather than straight. Nastaʿlīq was frequently incorporated into the paintings of the early Safavid period (in the sixteenth century), and is traditionally considered to be the most elegant of the Persian scripts. It is sometimes used to write Arabic-language text, but its use has always been more popular in Persian, Turkic, Urdu and other South Asian scripts. Nastaʿlīq has extensively been, and still is, practised in Iran, Pakistan and Afghanistan for writing poetry and as a form of art.

5. The Kufic is the oldest calligraphic form of the various Arabic scripts and consists of a modified form of the old Nabataean script.

6. A book written during Akbar's reign, it was and, still is, considered to be a standard work of book production. Shah Jahan's sons were trained calligraphers, using their skills to write letters and books. Prince Dara Shikoh, the eldest son of Shah Jahan, patronized master calligraphers and artists from Iran and Central Asia. Tughra, a style that creates animal forms with letters and texts, was executed by Dara Shikoh

7. Tariq Rehman, *From Hindi to Urdu: A Social and Political History* (Karachi: Oxford University Press, 2012).

8. John Windsor, 'Get some writing on your wall', *Guardian*, 12 November 2006; available online at http://www.theguardian. com/money/2006/nov/12/alternativeinvestment.india.

9. Brij Narayan Chakbast was an Urdu poet born in in Faizabad, near Lucknow, in January 1882, to a Kashmiri Pandit family. He was primarily a poet, but his prose is also considered at par with his poetry. This is a famous couplet on his description of life and death.

10. *Kakizome*, which, in Japanese means 'first writing', is traditional Japanese calligraphy written at the beginning

of the year or, more precisely, on 2 January annually. This tradition is also known as *Kitsusho Hajime*, or 'first fortune writing'.

Chapter 8: The Boat Makers of Balagarh

1. Shaista Khan eliminated the Portuguese who were frequently raiding trade ships and settlements near the Hooghly river. The Mughal naval forces were weak at this time and were often plundered by Portuguese pirates. Shaista Khan prepared a flotilla of around 300 boats from yards on the Hooghly and defeated the enemy and later developed a boat-building business in Dhaka in Tanti Bazaar. *See* Abhay Kumar Singh, *Modern World System and Indian Proto-Industrialization: Bengal 1650–1800*, volume 1 (New Delhi: Northern Book Centre, 2006); and Jaswant Lal Mehta, *Advanced Study in the History of Modern India, 1707–1813* (New Delhi: New Dawn Press Group, 2005).

2. 'In every part of His Majesty's empire, ships are numerous; but in Bengal, Kashmir, and T"hat'hah (Sindh) they are the pivot of all commerce. His Majesty had the sterns of the boats made in the shape of wonderful animals, and thus combines terror with amusement. Turrets and pleasing kiosks, markets, and beautiful flower-beds, have likewise been constructed on the rivers.' Abū'l-Fażl 'Allāmī, *The Ain i Akbari*, trans. H. Blochmann and H.S. Jarrett (Calcutta: Asiatic Society of Bengal, 1873).

3. The Rajbanshis are a community of fishermen belonging to a lower caste, according to the Hindu caste system. Most other boatmen who build boats do it with the help of the knowledge of these Rajbanshis. They often operate in Rajbanshi para, Sripur or Chandra Colony in Balagarh

along with other Muslim craftsmen. A lot of Brahmanic customs have filtered into this essentially non-Brahmanic community to ensure the sanctity of the boat-making craft and a wider economic reach catering to all castes and classes. For further reading on the tradition and culture of Rajbanshis and the boats made by them, *see* Swarup Bhattacharyya, 'Balagarhi Dinghi' in *Connected by the Sea: Proceedings of the Tenth International Symposium on Boat and Ship Archaeology, Denmark 2003*, ed. Lucy Blue et al. (Oxford: Oxbow Books, 2006).

4. A local spirit made from rice. Chullu production is a part of the culture and spiritual practices of the region. The recipe for it is, however, a secret and passed on orally from generation to generation.

5. Various editions of the *Manasha Mangal Kavya*, written around the fifteenth century, speak of a seafaring merchant Chand Sagar and the boat-making units in Saptagram. The word 'Saptagram' means seven villages. These are identified as Bansberia, Kristapur, Basudebpur, Nityanandapur, Sibpur, Sambachora and Baladghati. From the map of Van Don Broucke (1560 AD) it is quite clear that River Bhagirathi used to branch off into three streams near Triveni, on the Hooghly. But *Rennel's Atlas*, a century later, shows that the three streams had merged into one, more or less corresponding to the present-day river. In the process of shifting, it had abandoned Saptagram, and boats and ships could no longer reach here due to the river closing up. The boat-making units moved to the neighbouring village of Balagarh, whereas the trade activities moved to Calcutta. *See* Nitish Sengupta, *Land of Two Rivers* (London: Penguin Books UK, 2011).

6. *Clinker* built is a method of *boat* building where the edges of hull planks overlap.

7. Bhatiali, or Bhatiyali, is a form of folk music in Bengal. Bhatiyali is a boat song sung by boatmen while going downstream, as the word *bhatiyali* comes from *bhata*, meaning 'ebb' or 'downstream'. The boatmen also wrote ballads which were later set to music by village musicians. See Amaresh Datta, *Encyclopaedia of Indian Literature* (New Delhi: Sahitya Akademi, 1987).

Chapter 9: The Ittar Wallahs of Hyderabad

1. The Charminar is a monument and mosque located in Hyderabad. It was built by Muhammad Quli Qutb Shah in 1591 to commemorate the eradication of the plague. He had prayed for the end of the plague that was destroying his city and had vowed to build a mosque at the very place where he prayed.

2. The Char Kaman, built in 1592 by Sultan Muhammad Quli, are four arches at a distance of about 75 metres from the Charminar. All four arches are equidistant from each other. They served as a gateway to the palaces or other structures of royal importance. The Char Kaman also had areas allocated for shops that functioned from inside the four arches, selling jewellery, ittar and even Irani chai. The heritage conservation committee of Hyderabad Metropolitan Development Authority claims that they cannot evict the occupants as they are not harming the monument.

3. Dakhni emerged in the Deccan Plateau during the 1300s. It is similar to Urdu and Khari Boli, a western Hindi dialect. It is the lingua franca for most Muslims of the Deccan and some non-Muslims of the region as well.

4. R. Nath, *Private Lives of the Mughals in India (1526–1803 AD)* (New Delhi: Rupa Publications, 2004).

5. Kayasth is a caste or community of Hindus. Kayasths are considered to be members of the literate scribe caste, and have historically acted as keepers of records and public accounts, writers and administrators of the state, serving as ministers and advisers in early medieval Indian kingdoms and the Mughal empire, and even held important administrative positions during the British Raj.

6. The Musi river, now a drying river, divides the city of Hyderabad in two halves—the old city and the new city.

7. Al Buraq is a mythical creature in the Koran, smaller than a mule and bigger than a donkey, described as a creature from the heavens which transported the prophets.

Chapter 10: The Bhisti Wallahs of Calcutta

1. 'Badshahs' here refer to Muhammad Shah and the kings ruling under him, according to the timeline and information provided by Nawazuddin. Muhammad Shah headed the fast-dilapidating Mughal dynasty in the early-seventeenth century. He was the grandson of the Mughal emperor Bahadur Shah I.

2. Samuel Murray, *Seven Legs Across the Seas: A Printer's Impressions of Many Lands* (General Books, 2012).

3. John Forbes Watson and John William Kaye, *People of India*, vol. IV (London: W.H. Allen and Co, 1868–1875).

4. Animal skins, as those of cows and buffaloes were considered sacred and, hence, it was considered unholy for Hindus to use water stored in the same.

5. Drum beaters are another set of fading ancient professionals who serve as human alarms, waking people up during the months of Ramadan for their morning prayers.

6. Tangra or China Town, once humming with more than 350 tanneries, is in decline due to the dwindling number of Chinese residents who ran the tanneries. The residents are now about 1200-odd, from the estimated 23,000 in the early-Independence years.

7. Soumitra Das, 'The Last Days of Gunga Din', *Telegraph*, 3 January 2010; available online at http://www.telegraphindia. com/1100103/jsp/calcutta/story_11934114.jsp.

Chapter 11: The Letter Writers of Bombay

1. A clause in the Posts and Telegraphs Manual states: 'In case of a large head office or its town sub-offices, the superintendent may, when he considers it advisable, lease out the right to use the post office premises for this purpose to a contractor . . . and is justifiable only when the interests of the public can be served, i.e., when it is possible thereby to secure trustworthy writers who will do the work at least as well and at as low rates as other professional writers.' Under the scheme, hundreds of professional letter-writers sat outside post offices across India, within the premises, writing letters for the illiterate and 'every post office will be supplied by the Superintendent with printed notices (MS-42) in English and the vernacular showing the fixed scale of fees.'

2. S.M. Street is Calicut was known to produce fountain pens and related paraphernalia. The production started in the early 1950s and still continues till today in a few shops.

3. Historian Najaf Haider says the katibs, or scribes, of the Mughal era were the predecessors of today's letter writers who wrote letters for kings and commoners. *See* 'Training

of a Clerical Elite in Peninsular India, c. 1300–1800',
Indian Economic and Social History Review 47, no. 4, Sage
Publications, 2010; and D.N. Jha, ed., *The Development
of a Nation: Essays in Memory of R.S. Sharma* (New Delhi:
Manohar Publications, 2014).

GLOSSARY

- adda

  The fusion of cups of tea and the endless exchange of words that provides intellectual stimulus, or just a spontaneous gathering that occurs recurrently with a similar set of people; the topic of interests may range from politics to movies to science.

- Aghoris

  Post-mortem ritual performers.

- Allah pak ki azmat se

  'It is the greatness of Allah'.

- alta

  Red pigment used to paint the hands and feet.

- atta

  Flour used for making rotis and breads.

- azan

  The Muslim call for prayer.

- babus

  They were the neo-urban rich Bengali men during the late-

	eighteenth and nineteenth centuries, fostered mostly by the zamindari system in the colonial Calcutta. In the modern world, the term refers to government officials.
◆ badam	Almond.
◆ bajra	Pearl millet.
◆ baksa	Suitcases.
◆ batasha	Semi-spherical white-coloured sugar-cakes.
◆ bhai	Brother.
◆ bhajan	A Hindu devotional song.
◆ Bhangi	A lower caste according to the Hindu caste system; even Dalit castes classed as backward such as the dhobi (washermen) are socially higher than the Bhangis, who are described as 'outcasts even amongst outcasts'.
◆ bhisti wallah	Water carrier.
◆ bichhoo	A scorpion.
◆ burka	A long piece of clothing that covers the face and body worn Muslim women.
◆ chakkar	Dizziness.
◆ chakki	A stone mill used for grinding.
◆ chameli ke phool	Jasmine flowers.

- charpoy — A light bedstead comprising a web of rope or tape netting.

- chela — A favoured servant.

- chillum — A hookah, or a small pipe used for smoking cannabis.

- chira — Bengali flattened rice.

- choli — A blouse.

- coolie — An unskilled labourer employed cheaply to lift heavy luggage.

- Dugar — A clan lineage.

- dumkuria — A shed with a hay roof and mud walls.

- elaichi — Cardamom.

- fakir — A Muslim religious ascetic who lives solely on alms.

- Ganga Maiyya — Goddess Ganga. *Maiyya* means 'mother'.

- ghats — A broad flight of steps leading down to the bank of a river in India, used especially by bathers.

- ghee — Clarified butter.

- ghungroo — Small metallic bells strung together to form a tinkling, musical anklet.

- gobar — Cow dung.

- gulab — Rose.

- hafta — Illegal use of one's official position or powers, mostly by goons and syndicates, to extort money.

- haleem — A Muslim delicacy, popular in Hyderabad, made of wheat, barley, meat (usually beef or mutton, but sometimes chicken or minced meat), lentils and spices, and slow-cooked for seven to eight hours.

- haveli — Mansions in the Indian subcontinent belonging originally to royalty, often with historical and architectural significance.

- huzoor — Respected sir.

- jajman — Customers.

- jihad — An Islamic term referring to the religious duty of Muslims to maintain the religion; in Arabic, the word *jihād* is a noun meaning 'to strive, to apply oneself, to struggle, to persevere'.

- jharokha — A type of overhanging enclosed balcony often seen in Rajasthani architecture.

- jubba — A long robe.

◆ Jum'ah	A congregational prayer that Muslims hold every Friday, just after noon in the place of *dhuhr*.
◆ kabootar	Pigeon.
◆ kabootarbaaz	Pigeon fliers.
◆ kabootarkhana	A house for pigeons, complete with dovecote.
◆ kaju	Cashewnut.
◆ khala	Father's sister.
◆ khandaani	Running in the family for generations.
◆ Khat	Script.
◆ khus-khus	Poppy seeds.
◆ khus	Vetiver.
◆ khushkhati	Calligraphy in Urdu.
◆ khushnavisi	Calligraphy as it is referred to in Persian.
◆ Kufic	The earliest extant Islamic style of the handwritten alphabet that was used by early Muslims to record the Koran.
◆ kul purohit	The title 'tirth purohit' or 'kul purohit' simply means 'priest of the pilgrimage centre'.
◆ kumkum	During the marriage ceremony, the groom applies a coloured powder, kumkum to

the parting of the bride's hair as a part of the Hindu marriage ceremony, signifying their marriage. Once widowed, a woman is not supposed to wear kumkum.

◆ kurta	Long sleeved hip-length upper garment worn in the Indian subcontinent.
◆ kushti	Wrestling.
◆ kutiya	A small hut.
◆ laddus	Balls of sweets made from various ingredients—the base being a mixture of sugar and shortening and then shaped into a ball.
◆ lajja	Modesty.
◆ lassi	A sweet or savoury yoghurt milk made with thick yogurt and water.
◆ lathi	A heavy pole or stick.
◆ Mahapatras	Funeral ritual performers.
◆ mandir	Temple.
◆ mashq	A traditional water-carrying bag, usually made of waterproofed goatskin, from North India.
◆ masjid	Mosque.
◆ mithai	Indian sweets.

◆ moksha	The emancipation or freedom from the cycle of death and rebirth (in terms of Hindu philosophy).
◆ Muharram	A month of mourning in remembrance of the martyrdom of Imam Hussein, the grandson of the Prophet Muhammad. Shiite Muslims flagellate themselves during a Muharram procession, often drawing blood from their bodies.
◆ mustahab	The duties recommended, but not essential, the fulfilment of which is rewarded, though they may be neglected without punishment.
◆ nana	Maternal grandfather.
◆ nasal	Breed.
◆ oath commissioner	A formal appointment or commission that governments give to individuals empowering them to certify the oath of another person upon documents such as affidavits.
◆ odhni	A dupatta or light stole.
◆ paan	A preparation of betel leaf together with betel nuts and

	lime. Upon being chewed, the combination produces red-coloured juices, staining one's mouth.
◆ paap	'Sin' in Hinduism.
◆ pak saaf(i)	To be clean (in terms of Islam).
◆ pandit	A Hindu scholar learned in Sanskrit and Hindu philosophy and religion; typically also a practising priest.
◆ panji	Extensive genealogical records maintained among the Maithil Brahmins, except that they were also expected to rote-learn the records.
◆ para	A Bengali term which means 'a neighbourhood', usually characterized by a strong sense of community.
◆ pie	One-sixth of a cent back when Samuel Murray first wrote the book in 1918.
◆ pitaji	Father.
◆ qalam	A type of thin, long pen made from a dried reed; used for Islamic calligraphy.
◆ qalamtrash	Scissors for the reed pen.

◆ qiblah	The direction of the Kaaba (the sacred building at Mecca), to which Muslims turn to during prayers.
◆ randi	A prostitute.
◆ rangoli	A folk art in which patterns are created on the floor in living rooms or courtyards using materials such as coloured rice, dry flour, coloured sand or flower petals.
◆ registan	Desert.
◆ roti	Flat bread.
◆ salan	A popular Hyderabadi dish, also known as *mirchi ka salan*, it has long deep-fried chillies in a gravy with a predominant flavour of peanuts, sesame and cumin.
◆ sangri	Khejri (*Prosopis cineraria*) fruits or pods are locally called *sangar* or *sangri*. Dried green sangri is used as a delicious dried vegetable, and the unripe sangri is used in the preparation of curries and pickles.
◆ sardar	A title used before the names of Sikh men.

◆ sarpanch   The village headman and the focal point of contact between government officers and the local community.

◆ shaukeen   Zealous fanciers of objects or things.

◆ shayari   Poetry.

◆ shubhraj   A poem or a speech delivered by the Manganiyars in praise of a jajman and his family to ensure their well-being and also, in a way, to remember their family lineage.

◆ Sundar hai na?   'Isnt it beautiful?'

◆ suniye   Listen.

◆ sura   A chapter of the Koran. There are 114 chapters in all, each divided into verses.

◆ tasbeeh   A set or string of prayer beads used by Muslims as a counting aid in reciting the titles of Allah and during meditation.

◆ tashreef laiye 'Please come in'.

◆ telivaina   'Brilliant' in Telugu.

◆ thakur   A feudal title that literally means 'lord' in Hindi. The word *thakurani* means the wife of a thakur. The big zamindars of yore often used thakur as their title or surname, and was also employed as the feudal title by rulers of the former princely states of India.

- tilak

  A mark worn by a Hindu on the forehead to indicate caste, status, sect, or as an ornament.

- toddy

  The naturally alcoholic sap of some kinds of palm, used as a beverage in tropical countries.

- tukda

  A set of pigeons usually trained together.

- tummeda

  The large black carpenter bee (in Telugu).

- ustad

  An expert or a highly skilled person.

- zaikedar

  Delicious.

- zarda

  Milk with rice noodles and nuts.

BIBLIOGRAPHY

Chapter 1: The Godna Artists of Jharkhand

1. Anderson, Clare. 'Godna: Inscribing Indian Convicts in the Nineteenth Century'. In *Written on the Body: The Tattoo in European and American History*, edited by Jane Caplan. London: Reaktion Books, 2000.
2. Chima, Jugdep S. *Ethnic Subnationalist Insurgencies in South Asia: Identities, Interests and Challenges to State Authority*. New York: Routledge, 2015.
3. Dr Saroj Rai and Rajendra Rai, the latter known as the Laal Sahib of the royal family of Ranchi, in discussion with the author, March, 2015.
4. Gupte, S. Gajrani. 'Notes on Female Tattoo Designs in India'. In *History, Religion and Culture of India, Volume 4*. 1902.
5. Patnaik, Nityananda. *Folklore of Tribal Communities: Oral Literature of the Santals, Kharias and Oraons*. New Delhi: Gyan Publishing House, 2002.

6. Peterson, John (Universität Leipzig). 'A Kharia–English Lexicon'. *Himalayan Linguistics* (0)1 (2009): https://escholarship.org/uc/item/4566c4bw.

7. Rao, C.H., 'Note on Tattooing in India and Burma', *Anthropos* 37 (1946): 175–79.

8. Roy, S.C. 'Birth and Childhood Ceremonies among the Oraons'. *Journal of the Bihar and Orissa Research Society* (1915).

9. Website: India: Land of Eternal Ink, Lars Krutak: http://www.vanishingtattoo.com/india_tattoo_history.htm.

Chapter 2: The Rudaalis of Rajasthan

1. Gahlot, Jagdish Singh Gahlot. *Rajasthan: A Socio-Economic Study.* Jodhpur: Rajasthan Sahitya Mandir, 1981.

2. Gupta, R.K. and Bakshi, S.R. *Studies in Indian History: Rajasthan through the Ages.* New Delhi: Sarup and Sons, 2008.

3. *Indian Journal of Social Development* 3.

4. Jamanadas, K. 'The Rajput Period Was Dark Age of India'. http://www.ambedkar.org/research/Rajput_Period_Was_Dark_Age_Of_India.htm.

5. Kapoor, Priya. 'Rudali (The Lamenter): Mourning as Cultural Practice'. Paper presented at the annual meeting of the International Communication Association. New Orleans, 27 May 2004.

6. Lutz, Tom. *Crying: The Natural and Cultural History of Tears.* New York: W.W. Norton & Company, 1994.

7. Sekher, Ajay. 'Gender, Caste and Fiction: A Bahujan Reading of Mahasweta Devi's Rudali'. *Economic and Political Weekly* 41, 42 (21–27 October 2006).

8. Singh, K.S. and Lavani, B.K., eds., *People of India: Rajasthan, Volume 1, Anthropological Survey of India*. New Delhi: Popular Prakashan, 1998.

Chapter 3: The Genealogists of Haridwar

1. Basu, Soma. *Salvation for Seers, Curse for Farmers. Down to Earth* (February 2013).
2. *Genealogical Journal* 1–5. Utah Genealogical Association, 1972.
3. Lochtefeld, James. *God's Gateway: Identity and Meaning in a Hindu Pilgrimage Place*. New York: Oxford University Press, 2010.
4. McKean, Lise. *Divine Enterprise: Gurus and the Hindu Nationalist Movement*. Chicago: University of Chicago Press, 1996.
5. Menon, Dilip M. *Cultural History of Modern India*. New Delhi: Social Science Press, 2006.
6. Shoumatoff, Alex. *The Mountain of Names, Reporter at Large. New Yorker Magazine* (May 1985).

Chapter 4: The Kabootarbaaz of Old Delhi

1. 'Allāmī, Abū'l-Faẓl. *The Ain i Akbari*. Translated by H. Blochmann and H.S. Jarrett. Calcutta: Asiatic Society of Bengal, 1873.
2. Dalrymple, William. *City of Djinns: A Year in Delhi*. New Delhi: Penguin Books India, 2003.
3. Dayal, Maheshwar. *Rediscovering Delhi: The Story of Shahjahanabad*. New Delhi: S. Chand Publishing, 1975.

4. Eraly, Abraham. *Emperors of the Peacock Throne: The Saga of the Great Mughals*. New Delhi: Penguin Books India, 2007.

5. Greenberg, Joel. *A Feathered River Across the Sky: The Passenger Pigeon's Flight to Extinction*. New York: Bloomsbury USA, 2014.

6. *Marathon in the Sky: The Story of Pigeon Racing*. Directed by Jim Jenner. Paccom Films, 1990.

7. Monserrate, S.J. *The Commentary of Father Monserrate on His Journey to the Court of Akbar*. Translated by J.S. Hoyland. London: Humphrey Milford, Oxford University Press, 1922.

8. Mustard, Amanda. 'Finding Respite among Cairo's Pigeon Fanciers'. Interview by Janna Dotschkal. *National Geographic* (20 January 2015).

9. PETA. 'Investigation Exposes Pigeon-Racing Cruelty'. http://www.peta.org/features/pigeon-racing-investigation/

10. Rapson, Edward James, Haig, Wolseley and Bur, Richard. *The Cambridge History of India* 4. New Delhi: S. Chand Publishing, 1963.

Chapter 5: The Storytellers of Andhra

1. Brandon, James R., ed. *The Cambridge Guide to Asian Theatre*. Cambridge: Cambridge University Press, 1993.

2. Dhanaraju, Vulli. 'The Telangana Movement (1946–1951): Folklore Perspective'. *International Journal of Social Science Tomorrow* 1, no. 8 (2012).

3. Kaushal, Molly. *Chanted Narratives: The Living 'Katha-Vachana' Tradition*. New Delhi: Indira Gandhi National Centre for the Arts, 2001.

4. Varadpand, Manohar Laxman. *History of Indian Theatre* 2. New Delhi: Abhinav Publications, 1992.

Chapter 6: The Street Dentists of Baroda

1. Constable, Nicole, ed. *Guest People: Hakka Identity in China and Abroad*. Seattle: University of Washington Press, 1996.
2. Khu, Josephine M.T., ed. *Cultural Curiosity: Thirteen Stories about the Search for Chinese Roots*. Berkeley and Los Angeles, California: University of California Press, 2001.
3. Ozihel, Harding. *Street Dentistry*. Frac Press, 2012.
4. Seccombe, Karen and Hoffman, Kim. *Just Don't Get Sick: Access to Health Care in the Aftermath of Welfare Reform*. New Brunswick, New Jersey: Rutgers University Press, 2007.
5. Sircar, D.C. *Studies in the Geography of Ancient and Medieval India*. New Delhi: Motilal Banarsidass Publishers, 1990.
6. Woodforde, John. *The Strange Story of False Teeth*. New York: Universe Books, 1968.

Chapter 7: The Urdu Scribes of Delhi

1. Asher, Frederick M. and Gai, Govind Swamirao. *Indian Epigraphy: Its Bearing on the History of Art*. New Delhi: Oxford and IBH Publishing Company and the American Institute of Indian Studies, 1985.
2. Bhutta, Muhammad Iqbal. 'Muslim Calligraphy in the Subcontinent'. Nazaria-i-Pakistan Trust. Website: http://www.nazariapak.info/Research-corner/Calligraphy-sub.php.
3. Hamker, Susan Miyagi. Kakizome: The First Writing of the New Year'. JapanCulture.NYC (4 January 2013). Website: http://www.japanculture-nyc.com/2013/01/04/japanculture%E2%80%A2nycs-kakizome-the-first-writing-of-the-new-year/.

4. Madhu, Manjusha. 'The Art of Devotion and a Devotion to Art'. *Sunday Guardian*, 20 May 2012. Website: http://www.sunday-guardian.com/artbeat/the-art-of-devotion-a-a-devotion-to-art.

5. Rahman, Mustafizur. *Islamic Calligraphy in Medieval India*. Bangladesh: University Press Ltd, 1979.

6. Srivastava, R.P. *Art and Archaeology of Punjab*. New Delhi: Sundeep Parkashan, 1990.

7. Website of the Urdu Academy: http://urduacademydelhi.com/.

Chapter 8: The Boat Makers of Balagarh

1. Behera, K.S., ed. *Maritime Heritage of India*. New Delhi: Aryan Books International, 1999.

2. Bera, Gautam Kumar et al., eds. *In the Lagoons of the Gangetic Delta*. New Delhi: Mittal Publications, 2010.

3. Bhattacharyya, Swarup. 'Balagarhi Dinghi'. In *Connected by the Sea: Proceedings of the Tenth International Symposium on Boat and Ship Archaeology, Denmark 2003*, edited Lucy Blue et al. Oxford: Oxbow Books, 2006.

4. Datta, Rangan. 'Sripur: Temples and Boats' (19 February 2012). Website: https://rangandatta.wordpress.com/2012/02/19/sripur-temples-boats/.

5. Deloche, Jean. 'Boats and Ships in Bengal Terracotta Art'. *Bulletin de l'Ecole française d'Extrême-Orient* 78, no. 2 (1991).

6. Eaton, Richard M. *The Rise of Islam and the Bengal Frontier, 1204–1760*. California: University of California Press, 1993.

7. Eaton, Richard Maxwell. *The Rise of Islam and the Bengal Frontier, 1204–1760*. California: University of California Press, 1996.

8. Hornell, James. 'The Origin and Ethnological Significance of Indian Boat Designs' in *Memoirs of the Asiatic Society of Bengal*. Calcutta, 1920.
9. James, Renell. *Memoirs of a Map of Hindoostan*. London, 1792.
10. Mohaka, Payal. *The Shadow: Unknown Craftsmen of Bengal*. New Delhi: Niyogi Books, 2007.

Chapter 9: The Ittar Wallahs of Hyderabad

1. Beveridge, Henry, ed. *The Tuzuk-i-Jahangiri; or Memoirs of Jahangir*. Translated by Alexander Rogers. London: London Royal Asiatic Society, 1909.
2. Kapoor, J.N. 'Attars of India: A Unique Aroma'. *Perfumer & Flavorist* (January/February 1991): pp. 21–24.
3. Kaviratna, Avinash Chunder, trans. *Samhita: Handbook on Ayurveda Part 1*. 1896.
4. Krishnamurthy, R. 'Perfumery in Ancient India'. *Indian J Hist Sci*. 22, no. 1 (January 1987): pp. 71–79.
5. McHugh, James. *Sandalwood and Carrion: Smell in Indian Religion and Culture*. New York: Oxford University Press USA, 2012.
6. Mcmohan, Christopher. 'Indian Attars'. *International Journal of Aromatherapy* 7, no. 4 (1996): pp. 10–13.
7. RVS. 'Quaint Corner: The Scents of 'Ind' and Their Fragrance'. *Statesman*. 1 August 2013. Website: http://www.thestatesman.com/news/8307-quaint-corner-the-scents-of-ind-160-and-their-fragrance.html.
8. Smith, R.V. 'The scent in the wind!' *The Hindu*. 13 February 2012. Website: http://www.thehindu.com/todays-paper/tp-features/tp-metroplus/the-scent-in-the-wind/article2886872.ece.

9. Yemul, Omprakash. 'India Where Attars Originated'. *India Perspectives* (March 2004): p. 40.

Chapter 10: The Bhisti Wallahs of Calcutta

1. Durand, Ralph Anthony. *A Handbook to the Poetry of Rudyard Kipling*. New York: Doubleday, Page Company, 1914.

2. Ghosh, T. and Nath S. *People of India: Delhi, Volume XX (Anthropological Survey of India)*. New Delhi: Manohar Publishers, 1996.

3. Kanher, Usha Shashikant. *Women and Socialisation: A Study of Their Status and Role in Lower Castes*. New Delhi: Mittal Publications, 1987.

4. Lal, Ananda. *The Oxford Companion to Indian Theatre*. New Delhi: Oxford University Press, 2004.

5. Limb, Sue and Cordingley, Patrick. *Captain Oates: Soldier and Explorer*. London: Batsford Ltd, 1982.

6. Russell, R.V. and Hiralal. *The Tribes and Castes of the Central Provinces of India*. London: Macmillan, 1916.

7. Tharoor, Shashi. *The Great Indian Novel*. New York: Arcade Publishing, 2011.

8. Wells, Jeremy. *Romances of the White Man's Burden: Race, Empire, and the Plantation in American Literature*. Nashville, Tennessee: Vanderbilt University Press, 2011.

A NOTE ON THE AUTHOR

A young journalist based out of Calcutta, Nidhi Dugar Kundalia is an MA from City University, London. She has written extensively on society, subcultures and cultural oddities in newspapers like *The Hindu*, the *Times of India* and magazines like *Kindle Magazine* and *Open*. This is her first book.